Praise for *Dear Jo*

'A must read'

'In this outrageous spoof a filth-strewn look at sex, rela... and why women are always in the wrong when marriages crumble - brilliant comedians Vicki Pepperdine and Julia Davis have excelled themselves in their roles as the chillingly convincing agony aunts Joan and Jericha. Their award-winning podcast now runs to two series, and if you're already a fan, the advice offered in this book, from dating to death, will come as no surprise. Brace yourself? for a bumpy ride. The darkest and dirtiest of humour, not for the faint-hearted' Woman & Home

'Fans of the outrageous, satirical agony aunts will love this spin off book' Red Magazine

'A stunningly explicit guide to finding, keeping and pleasing a man, littered with sex advice and personal revelations' Heat Magazine

'An impossibly funny treat' Grazia

WHY HE TURNS AWAY

Do's and Don'ts, from Dating to Death

Joan Damry and Jericha Domain

First published in Great Britain in 2020 by Trapeze,
This paperback edition published in 2021 by Trapeze,
an imprint of The Orion Publishing Group Ltd
Carmelite House, 50 Victoria Embankment,
London EC4Y 0DZ

An Hachette UK company

1 3 5 7 9 10 8 6 4 2

A CIP catalogue record for this book is available from the British Library.

ISBN (Mass Market Paperback) 9781398700604

Printed and bound in Great Britain
by Clays Ltd, Elcograf, S.p.A.

www.orionbooks.co.uk

Joan Damry was born in Galbraith, Scotland, one of nine children crammed happily into a two-up two-down with an outside toilet. Joan entered the world feet first, the umbilical cord wrapped tightly around the top of her head like a fleshy turban, leaving her with a cone-shaped skull, which is why she continues to wear her hair high. Devoted mother of five and wife to coma-bound husband Ralph, Joan is also a life coach, psychogenital counsellor, much admired TED-talk speaker, accomplished flautist and writer of best-selling erotic fiction series Lust and Lies at *Glanmore Manor*. Joan has been married six times, three of her husbands having tragically taken their own lives.

Jericha Domain is proud to be British. Dedicated mother and tender wife (though her husband Philip spends 98% of his time running a Boy Scout school in Thailand), Jericha is also an award-winning writer having penned five books on depression, and another entitled *Wild Lady Swims: A guide to Britain's Most Polluted Waterways*. A keen front crawler, Jericha is often seen pounding up and down the Regent's Canal, dodging oncoming craft in her russet tankini and homemade flippers. Jericha divides her days between broadcasting, writing, lecturing, gardening and liaising with the police regarding her adult daughter Cardinal.

Contents

Dear reader,

Welcome to what we feel sure you'll find is an unputdownable sex and relationships bible to guide you through what's left of your life. It has been our unrelenting mission to help all the lost lady lambs, especially old muttony ones, that fumble through life in too-tight trousers and a clumpy shoe, looking for love in all the wrong places. Herewith, we proffer a step-by-step, medically approved manual on how to meet, marry and keep a husband. Along the way you will find quizzes, tips, recipes, letters and our own personal stories that we are kindly sharing for the sake of your happiness. Why? Because God gave us a gift.

We both knew from an early age that we were healers. Healers don't always come in gypsy skirts, with claggy eye make-up and jewellery made from forks. Sometimes they are a sassy Scotch babe in a mini-kilt, with thigh-high Dick Whittington boots and big-nippled boobs. Sometimes they are a broad-shouldered, high-haired mum to a large-headed lesbian, pounding up Regent's Canal in a russet tankini and homemade flippers, gulping down murky, infected water.

So heal we must, because when the final curtain comes down on our lives, we know we can rest easy in the knowledge that we gave, and we gave, and we gave again. Our room is booked, thank you very much, in the Heaven Hotel. We know there's a kettle, we know there are biccies, and we know there will be no businessman's botty smudges on our white linen sheets, because we have chosen to devote ourselves to the pairing up of others, and this will be our life's great legacy.

'Reader, I married him,' said the wonderful, though rather plain, Charlotte Brontë (who finally managed to bag a hubby only to pass away a few months later, which may well happen to you if you're not careful) and indeed our heartfelt prayer is that this little book can help you not only to achieve every girl's dream of dreams, but also give hubby enough reasons to stay with you for as long as he can possibly bear it.

And remember, if things don't work out, you only have yourself to blame.

Warmest wishes,

Joan Damry and Jericha Domain

Chapter 1

WHY HE TURNS AWAY

Getting Yourself Hubby Body Ready

Sadly, many of you reading this book will be large, lonely, rather whiffy spinsters of a certain age: dumpy, dowdy, often balding, but still desperate to find Mr Right. Perhaps you're still living at home with Mum, promising her your prince is on his way as you gobble down your fourth sausage roll and embroider yet another flower onto your giant wedding dress.

Were you a dumpy, dowdy, balding *guy* of a similar age, the story would be very different. There would be a queue of luscious lasses eager to un-pop their slutty brassieres, whip off their panties and hop aboard your lumpy love train. Of course, we would dearly love to help each and every one of you to find a husband, but the unavoidable truth is we are now living in the midst of an unprecedented epidemic. That of ...

The Prowling Spinster

These are women much like yourself, who are well past their sell-by date (often in their thirties and beyond) who simply refuse to hang up their sex boots and throw in the towel.

With fingers worn to nubs through frenzied swiping on all their dirty dating apps, their homes a veritable war zone of crispy gussets and ravaged sex toys, these frantic frumps are forever on the trouser-prowl, looking, lurking, loitering. If they're not simpering around supermarkets, or bumping their big bottoms too close to guys in libraries, they will be parading around nice market towns with their mouths wide open, trying to give married men blow jobs. Or when in cosmopolitan London, stuffing their desperate fingers down the back of men's trews on crowded underground trains.

For all you sad Spinsterellas, the bald fact is that you're unlikely to ever secure an actual husband, but since you won't go down without a fight, we are obliged to guide you towards the unusual types of men who may be willing to accept more than a passing trouser-browse, indeed a trouser-rouse and possibly some actual penile contact, however brief and unsavoury.

TOP TIPS FOR UNUSUAL VENUES TO MEET UNUSUAL GUYS!

- Your Own Doorstep. Next time the Amazon delivery guy calls round, answer the door in just your pants and ask him if he wants a cup of tea or 'something stronger'. Then, when he hands you the machine to sign for your parcel, grab at his crotch and say you'd like to sign for *his* parcel. He likely won't get the innuendo, but that's when you can make your move and haul him into your property. If you need to strike him with a blunt instrument, then so be it; a rolling pin works well, or simply bonk him to the ground with his own machine. And if he's unconscious for any length of time, it gives you the chance to test out the goods with a few dry humps and some long sloppy kisses. Should he come round mid-snog, explain that he had a massive heart attack and you're kindly administering life-saving mouth to mouth. You'd be surprised how many women have found a husband this way – many of them Hollywood celebrities like Gwyneth Paltrow.*

- The Doctors. Make as many appointments with male GPs as possible and no matter the ailment, always ask for an internal. Don't take no for an answer. This can work just as well with

* Fun fact, both Chris Martin and Brad Falchuk were Amazon delivery guys before marrying Gwyn and still keep their hand in now..

dentists as they are medically trained, so asking for an intimate examination is not out of the question – and wonderfully erotic if he keeps one glove on to fumble around your mouth and his naked hand to manipulate his pointy teeth-tools and poke his tiny mirrors about your front bottom.

- Maternity Wards. Maybe your best friend has just had a baby, so her husband will be desperate for sex. Now's the time to swoop in. Arrive at the hospital in thigh-high boots with your nipples erect and give her the small gift you've brought for baby (a second-hand hat or simple pen will suffice as babies really don't need much). Say she looks awful and ask how ARE her thirty stitches down below, then suggest you and 'Dad' grab a coffee from the hospital vending machine. Shovel him into the nearest cupboard en route and fellate him til the charge nurse knocks on the door for fresh linen supplies. You can then blackmail him by announcing you'll tell his wife he assaulted you and if he doesn't leave her and the new baby right now, you'll kill yourself. Works every time.

- Funerals can be a fab place to meet guys. And the beauty is you can gatecrash as many as you like, as no one will ever confront a weepy stranger in a sexy black number, particularly if she's let everyone know she's gone commando by sitting at the side and scissoring her legs throughout the service. A lot of these tragic mourning guys are very vulnerable, particularly if their wife has just passed away, as they don't know who's going to cook their dinner. Studies have shown that the human sex drive increases by 750 per cent at a funeral, particularly in the poignant moment when the coffin is just beginning to nudge its oaky head through the curtains at a cremation. This is the moment our scissoring lady can relish the sight of rows of gents with big bulgy frontages popping up along the pews. And at the reception afterwards there'll be many a locked cupboard and 'engaged' toilet sign, as dowdy spinsters with black lips from too much red wine disappear for twenty minutes, only to return with their jowly cheeks caked in creamy streaks. Folk enjoying the bereavers-buffet will suddenly find themselves bombarded by all sorts of fishy smells and wafts coming from those just back from the loos, the stench of mourner's sperm and 'Spinster's Vagina' hanging heavy in the air. So if you play your cards right funeral-wise, you might just end up with a ring on your finger for your troubles!

- Hospitals are also a great venue to nab a fella. You'll need to go for guys who are feeling desperate, so do keep your eyes peeled for someone who's just been told their wife is dying, or that they *themselves* are. Some of you may cock your snook at the thought of dating a dying guy, but beggars can't be choosers and at least you can show friends and family that you've finally got someone to call your own! It's also going to be a lot easier to force a terminal fella into marriage. But do hurry, because lonely ladies love to flock around a man on his last legs! Don't slack on grooming yourself, nor on pleasuring him – seal the deal in a chemo session with a hearty blow job and a couple of packets of Monster Munch. Some ladies don't want friends to know she's marrying a terminal guy, but with some heavy make-up and clever padding he can be made to look relatively normal so you can enjoy the big day as every woman should. When he does finally pop off, you can say, 'Just my luck!' or, 'I'd finally found Mr Right and now it's all gone wrong', and then you can angle for a luxury funeral shower, demanding a big batch of pricey sympathy gifts. There, you can brag about your perfect 'once in a lifetime' love, whilst keeping your eyes peeled at the cremation for any spare mourning hotties.

- Psychiatric hospitals are teeming with available guys, so all you desperate ladies who are normally at home with your dildos on constant charge can simply wander in and get amongst it to satisfy your grim fantasies. Security is very lax, so you can pose as a concerned relative or dress up as a sexy doctor – and with access to so many extremely powerful drugs and fun restraining aids, the world is your oyster! If you're in the mood, you can even 'kidnap' a new life partner (or take two home if you're feeling greedy!). Yes, there may be some teething issues with these unstable types trying to stab you or thinking they're Hitler but, let's face it, that's not much different from being married to a 'normal' guy!

- Death Row. Who doesn't love a bad guy? And here you've got hulking great beasts who've slaughtered their way to the electric chair, caged and dangerous, in this incredibly charged and romantic setting, having thus far only had each other for solace in the showers. It really is a huge turn-on for everyone involved as you flirt with your grisly killer on the phone and press your urgent breasts against the smeary glass panel, whilst the beefy prison guard looks on, a hefty bump forming in his greasy nylon trousers. But, ladies, this can be a competitive arena, so do be sure you're offering something a little bit more than all the other rabid spinsters foaming at the mouth in the booths alongside. Again, no pants please, if you want your murderer to propose!

- Isolated places. Women are generally told to avoid woods and deserted moors, but these can be wonderful ways to meet unusual men if you're down on your marital luck. Don't be too snobby if the guys you meet in the dead of night in a bleak wood or on a lonely moor are naked from the waist down, or are busy hanging hooks and nooses about the place. These are creative men who deserve your time and effort. You could make him feel more appreciated by whipping off your undies and tossing a trail of yummy biccies or gingerbread crumbs about the place and see if that doesn't have him running through the trees towards you with a big smile and a fat willy.

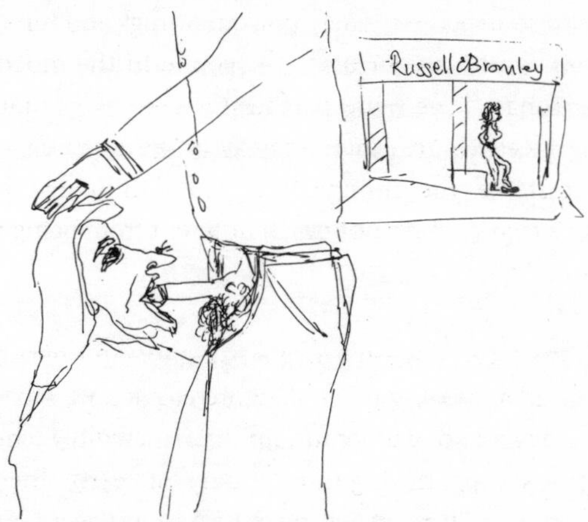

- Street corners. Finally, when all else has failed, your request can be as bald as standing on a street corner and shouting, 'Does anyone want to have sex with me?' Some men will pretend they don't want to because they're out shopping with their wives, agreeing with her muttered assertions that you must be mentally ill and so on. But the minute she's popped back to Russell & Bromley for a second look at those snaffle loafers, he'll be sniffing round you with his wet tongue lolling. That's your cue to haul him into the nearest disabled toilets and knock him out with your boobs until he agrees to divorce his snaffle-loafered incumbent.

Good luck!

How Do I Get A Husband If I'm Relatively Attractive?

Now to those of you thankfully still under thirty, you may yet be in with a chance to win at Love's Lottery and bag the hubby of your dreams. But you must act quickly! Men are, quite rightly, pretty choosy when it comes to picking a permanent penetration pal, so you will need to shape up or ship out!

Here we take you through a guide to grooming yourself top to bottom and getting yourself truly:

Hubby Body Ready!

Guys NEED to look at nice things: lovely leggy ladies with long luscious hair, big bouncy boobs and a tiny, bald vulva. But for most of you it's unlikely you have even *one* of the above, let alone that magic trio!

HAIR: LONG 'N' LUSH

So, let's start with hair! Be you a bold conker brunette or a butter-bean blonde, a guy needs lengthy locks to sweep across his genitals, flick over his moobs and whoosh around his sweaty face throughout your bawdy bonkathon. He'll love you lacing your hair around his proud penis, giving him a tufty maypole to yank about and generally have some fun with.

He'll also enjoy it if you pipe it up his anus – simply fashion it into a plait and stuff it up there, using it like a fun hairy dildo, and he'll be in heaven (with the added bonus of sweeping off old bits of impacted faeces that may have lodged in his rectum. As we know, guys rarely wipe their bottoms!).

Obviously we have both been blessed with firm, fat follicles bursting with horse-strong hair, managed by our wonderful hairdressers Mick and Mark.*

If you don't have long hair then grow it, ladies, for goodness sake! But for those of you with female pattern baldness or a face that is frankly too haggard to sport a long hairstyle, wigs are not advisable as he'll likely think you have a terminal illness.

BOOBS: BIG 'N' BOUNCY

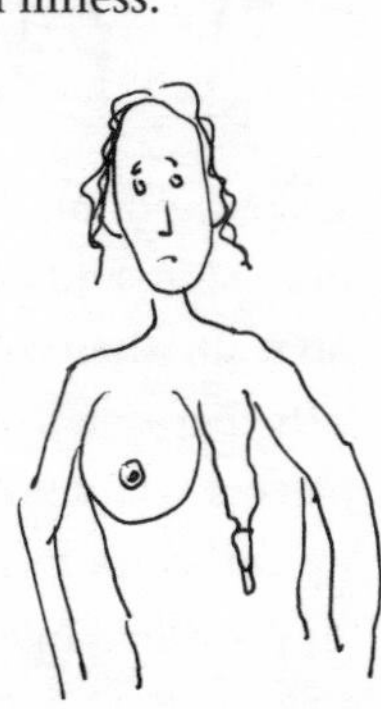

Many of you will have boobs that are simply too small. Or perhaps you boast one big one, but the other is just a dangly old broad bean. So what is the answer?

SURGERY.

Yes, surgery is *always* the answer, but many of you still kick up a stink about forking out for some nice big chest balls or a completely remoulded frontal botty, which frankly could mean the difference between a life as a successful married lady or a life alone.

* See Appendix B.

So how to get hold of the wonga? Well, let's say you're a fourteen-year-old girl. NOW is the time to be thinking about surgery and all your pocket money should be going into your special surgery jar. For inspiration, Mahmoud, our dear friend and world-famous cosmetic surgeon, does a wonderful range of surgery-inspired piggy banks:

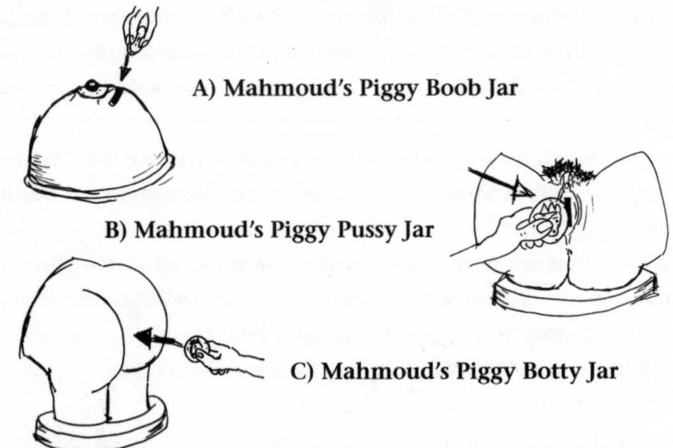

A) Mahmoud's Piggy Boob Jar

B) Mahmoud's Piggy Pussy Jar

C) Mahmoud's Piggy Botty Jar

This type of fund should really be getting contributions from birth from Mum and Dad, but also from godparents and interested uncles. After all, when babies are born they tend to be given all these ghastly gifts they don't need – cuddly toys, engraved spoons, clothes. So as parents you need to say, 'We don't want birth gifts, thank you, but we are accepting donations to little Celia's Bouncy Boob Jar.'

It's a bit of fun and people can choose their favourite body parts to splash out on. Uncles often give generously to the Piggy Boob Fund, whilst practical aunts will be eager to donate to the Long Leggy Piggy. Even male neighbours, recently widowed or troubled guys who live alone (and may be on a register but tend to be very pleasant), are often more than willing to invest a little something in the Piggy Pussy Jar. So why not organise a big boozy baby shower and, with some dirty flirting from Mum and a few bottles of fizzy wine, you can grab some serious wonga off these horny, lost and lonely fellas.

It especially cheers the elderly menfolk, decaying in their Parker Knoll armchairs, to think of their last pennies going towards some big bowling-ball boobs bobbing past their window in a few years' time, knowing they had a hand in building them. Or of that perfect piggy bank pussy they can catch a glimpse of when the wind blows up young Celia's netball skirt. These guys feel a great sense of ownership after donating towards these enhanced body parts and may even request they take them for a spin at some point which, frankly, wouldn't be unreasonable. And just as when one sponsors a monkey and you get a photo with the caption 'This is your orangutan, he's called Charlie', so dribbly old Eric from number 5 should get pics of Celia's wonderful emerging boobs – plus perhaps some bonus shots of botties, front or back – to keep him and all the generous menfolk on side.

But if you've left this all too late and you're now past thirty with only two sorry flaps to fill your bra, then please don't make the mistake of wearing these ghastly padded bras, as frankly, this is a criminal offence. It's not going to do what it says on the tin, because there's nothing in the tin! And we've seen many a man punch a wall when he's got a lady home, pinged off her padded brassiere, groped at what he'd been led to believe was a decent handful, only to find himself grasping at some air with a wart.

A final note on boob grooming: nipple hair. We're seeing far too many ladies walking about brandishing their hooters, proud as punch, with an unsightly ring of nipple pubes poking through their blouses. And they wonder why they are sans hubby!

Do keep it plucked, ladies, so your guy can go in for a suckle without gagging on your bristles. Nobody wants a big mouthful of wiry old hair on wrinkled skin – except for us gals when we're gobbling away at hubby's yummy scrotal package!

But all is not lost if surgery really isn't an option. There are some foods that do have an effect on chest size, which until now have been kept secret. For bigger boobs read on …

JOAN'S HOT HOCK HASH (FOR BIGGER BOOBS)

I love spicy food and this yummy dish is a real boob-booster. My boobs doubled in size whilst staying with Antonio Banderas on his ranch after he introduced me to this recipe and I think if my husband Ralph* hadn't been there something definitely would have happened, as Antonio couldn't keep his eyes off my chest and kept walking past me in his increasingly bulgy pants.

INGREDIENTS

You'll need:

A Scottish lamb (ideally Glaswegian; Edinburgh lambs tend to be a bit stand-offish)

6 scotch bonnet chillies

A clutch of dawn-plucked heather

A handbag-size bundle of yummy tatties

A big man's handful of turnips

One pint of Joan's 'Secret Oil' (available online at exclusive outlets)

---

* See Appendix B.

METHOD

Strip down to a glittery basque, pop on some Supertramp and start hashing all the ingredients together whilst rocking your pelvis to the beat, then toss into a deep frying pan, fill to the brim with Joan's secret oil and whack up the gas! Once sizzly, pipe the hot hash into your long hock-pot and roast overnight, allowing all the flavours to intercourse until morning.

Serve in a babydoll nighty with a big cappuccino and some salty cream-dippers.

Antonio and I stayed up for hours eating our way through his hot hock hash and I've honestly never felt more beautiful. Something about the sensual sharing of this dish, using just our fingers (his were quite stumpy), his rich Spanish timbre and smiling cocoa eyes brought out my inner goddess and I know I cast my spell on him. I just wish Ralph hadn't been there. He had his first giant stroke on the plane over and we thought he'd gone, but no.

Until now I haven't spoken about my 'Secret Oil', but I was first gifted it by Melvyn Bragg on a writing retreat in Tuscany where I was working on my third novella, *Lust and Lies At Glanmore Manor*. Melvyn's known for his big bouncy barnet, and I spied him one evening spraying this gorgeous gold mist onto his hair, after tonging it for dinner. I slipped into his bedroom in my crocheted bikini, showed him one of my dirty poems and asked if I could have a wee spritz. Melvyn was still in his sopping wet trunks and heeled holiday-crocs and the atmosphere was frankly electric. He started hazing me with his fine yellow mist, his eyes roving my lips as he soaked my face, hair and hot, throbbing bod, pushing the canister in and out of my mouth, almost dancing as he did it, his big hair bouncing – and God, it tasted like heaven. Like angel's tears, mixed with Bacardi. That night he told me he would name it after me and I've used it ever since.

THE PERFECT UNDERCARRIAGE (OR HOW TO HAVE A HOTTY'S BOTTY FRONT AND BACK!)

Guys love a pert, peachy bubblebutt at the back and a gorgeous, barely there vulva at the front. Medically these are known as Botty One and Botty Two. Joan's had the joy of a whole vulval transplant donated to her by a troubled teen and it really is stunning (and she won't mind me saying, much smaller than her original!). But for a lot of you, this is just too pricey, and we can't all wait around for someone to be run over. So what is the ideal vulva?

Small and bald!

If we look to the wonderfully sexy dolls developed by large sweaty guys in the 1970s, we are struck by her huge boobs, tiny waist and just a smudge of a vulva, in a nice, welcoming flamingo pink. Thanks, guys, for showing us what you want! Because let's face it, how often IRL do these poor guys get downstairs only to find a big old boiled beef-tomato vagina and then are so devastated they're unable to perform? They need a simple, understated slot to pump themselves into, in a baby pink or gauzy gold, nestling between the young lady's prised-open thighs.

But what if your vulva's a big droopy old squirrel that's constantly trying to escape your undies but you can't afford surgery? Fear not! Help is at hand with:

Joan and Jericha's
HOME
LABIAPLASTY
KIT!

Make an evening of it and sculpt your downstairs department into the type of yummy entrance that's going to make any guy want to slip his shoes off, step inside, and hopefully stay the night – **AND ALL FROM THE COMFORT OF YOUR OWN HOME!** Chop, tweak and sizzle off any unsightly Panty Bacon with our unique blow torch and alcohol combo, creating a mini groinal house fire that will singe away those flappy bits!

(Note: paracetamol is included for the over-sensitive amongst you!)

So crack open the fizzy wine, pop the Pringles, and let's get to it, ladies!

So assuming you've either had surgery or you've used our Home Labiaplasty kit, you'll now have your perfect, stunning, scar tissuey, clumpy pink, waxworky slot – but hang on! The inner workings are a hopeless baggy mess with a big old dangly clitoris to boot. There are exercises to tone and tidy this area and little girls can do this if they look likely to have a particularly rotund or tubby clitoris (and Mum has been too stingy to get the in-utero clit-tuck surgery).

However, no amount of stretching and weightlifting will shrink a real dangler. In that situation, rather like treating a wart, you'll need to buy a product that will essentially freeze the swinging clitoris right off. You won't be left with much – if any – feeling, but at least it won't look like a ghastly stalactity bulb drooping down between your knees.

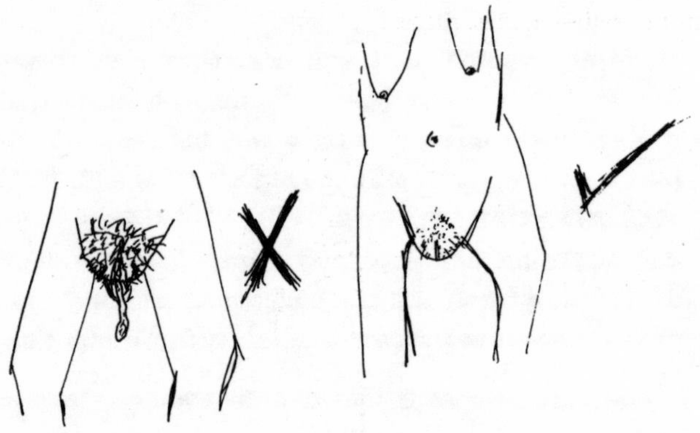

By this stage you should be feeling fairly confident having addressed issues with hair, boobs and vulvas. But ladies! Let's have a quick peep at our:

BACK BOTTIES

Botty Two, colloquially known by GPs as the 'back botty', needs to be toned, taut 'n' tasty if you want to attract and keep a hubby interested in playing hide the sausage in the bike rack. Let's look at how to groom in and around the area for those of you who have failed to keep it peachy perfect.

COTTAGE CHEESE: Cellulite is a big no-no for guys. With all the gorgeous lady booty on Pornhub for him to pump his lump to, it's going to be very hard for him to become aroused by your dimply botty cheeks and ghastly puckered thighs. If you don't have time to get liposuction before the date, do keep your back botty covered and wear crotch-high boots to keep the bulk of your legs hidden and squashed away. Guys love having sex with women in boots. But no wellies, ladies, please!

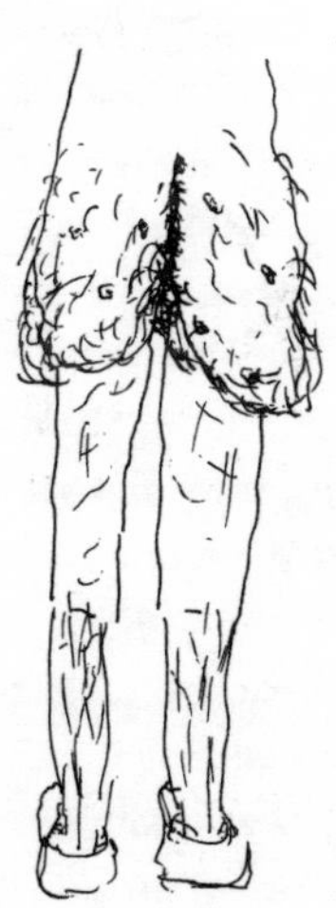

HAIRY BOTTOMS: Some lasses have a lot of hairs dotted around their botty cheeks. If you've failed to maintain your grooming schedule and are on an unexpected date, you will need to box a bit clever with your bum fur and make it appear that you are simply wearing a pair of textured panties. You can always slip to the restaurant loos and colour in between the hairs with a brown felt tip if need be. If you take a while colouring in your bottom, make sure your date doesn't think you did a number two as that's a grisly image he won't forget, so on your return explain there was a big queue, or better still, that someone died in the next cubicle.

ANAL BLEACHING: Ladies, please! We've talked time and again about the necessity of a pure white anus. Any woman walking around with anything stain-dark or dirty down there really deserves to be shot.

MIND THE GAP!: Thigh gaps are VITAL and should be ten to twelve inches ideally. The purpose of this thigh 'tunnel' is really for ease of penetration for the guys. It's a simple biological fact that if you've got big squashy thighs chafing together, your fella can barely squeeze himself up you. His testes will get trapped, the blood supply cuts off – and boom! Suddenly your guy is left with two dead raisins dangling from his chassis.

We had an incident like this very close to home, involving Stephanie,* Joan's galumphing PA. She'd somehow bulldozed this pleasant young gent, Alan, into making love to her after church one Sunday. Bear in mind Stephanie is a big, big girl and Alan was particularly slight. So there he was slapping back and forth, bless him, this tiny little man, whacking away trying to pleasure her, but she couldn't feel a thing because of all her doughy thigh-rolls. Alan pressed on regardless, but eventually got his testicles trapped in the bulk, which promptly sealed up, creating a dangerous vacuum. Stephanie rang 999, but by the time the paramedics arrived they

* See Appendix B.

had to actually cut poor Alan off her. Tragically for him, Stephanie was left with his near-dead testes trapped inside her thigh flesh and before long the wound started weeping semen. When he finally called round to collect his testes, she'd already milked off some love-juice, pushed it up inside herself and was now pregnant.

Stephanie is proudly walking around with his dead genitals lodged within her flesh, expecting the baby she'd always longed for, whilst Alan is left small and single, with only a pair of dangling fake plastic testes for his trouble. So in short we think you'll agree, a thigh gap is actually a medical emergency and requires urgent usage of:

GAPPY-GAL!

Joan and Jericha's hefty metal **thigh gap enhancer**, a contraption that must be worn all night and all day for six months for best results. The metal arm circles and stirs the fleshy area continuously, making it very sore and weepy, but spreading the thighs well apart. This eventually causes the thighs to essentially become afraid of each other, meaning that the excess flesh is then pushed out to the sides creating saddle bags, but guys don't mind grabbing on to a bit of that side-jiggle if they can have what they truly want – his beloved and vital thigh gap so he can pump til he dumps!

DISCLAIMER: This works best on long, modelly legs. If yours are stout and chunky, don't bother.

'GAPPY-GAL: FOR THE GIRL WHO HAS EVERYTHING BUT A HOLLOW BETWEEN HER THIGHS!'

COMPLETING THE TRANSFORMATION

When it comes to overall grooming, we often forget: guys love long nails! He wants those teasing talons driven deep and hard into his big wet back as he's bumping away on top, knowing his big grunty thrusts are driving you wild! And a quick shout out to our sapphic sisters here, because yes, they love a lengthy nail too! On her return recently from a weekend juggling course in Frome, my daughter Cardinal* surprised me with not only sporting a rather glossy feminine bob (instead of her usual angry mullet) but a banging set of big, shiny nails to boot, whose sudden growth she attributed to a wonderful recipe she had acquired after an interesting rendezvous on her train journey home ...

CARDINAL'S CHEESY SPRINGERS

JERICHA: Cardinal may be a drain on my life but goodness she has a way with fromage, and these calcium-packed Cheesy Springers have done wonders for my wiry pudendal hair, crumbly teeth and papery nails which were frankly just bald purple nubs for many years, on both finger and toe. Phillip also wolfs these Springers down on his rare visits home, when he's often covered in sores from his Far East travels and in need of a protein boost. Cardinal claims she got the recipe from Dame Judi Dench when the wonderful actress was stuck in the toilet on a train from Manchester to London, and Cardinal jimmied the lock, setting Dame Judi free. She then insisted Cardinal join her table and promptly released a very whiffy triangle which she called her 'cheesy springer', and insisted Cardinal have a good old munch.

* See Appendix B.

INGREDIENTS

You'll need:
An old brown loaf with just a rumour of mould
A clump of whey butter
A widow's clutch of spring onions
A large hunk of patched together cheeses from the back of the fridge
A large pack of calcium tablets from Holland & Barrett (dog ones will do if you don't have them)

METHOD

Mush all ingredients with a fork and form into a tennis-sized ball. Toss up and down to aerate, shiver on some flour and pop under the grill til sizzly.

Remove and triangulate using spatulas.

Serve with a boozy chutney and a crescent of crisps.

Enjoy! And marvel as your nails lengthen and curve into sexy shiny claws …

Mark, my aforementioned hairdresser, also loves these Springers and was able to gift me the feathery skullcap hairdo I'd so admired on Dame Judi since the early eighties. I'd managed to grab a somewhat blurry photo of her in Stratford-upon-Avon, when I saw her piling up her basket in the theatre gift shop (I think because she plays all those parts she's allowed to take whatever she wants), and I was so keen to ape the distinguished icon, I rushed out from the theatre, photo in hand and had a botch job done at what turned out to be a men's barbers, and left sporting a very severe buzz cut, with shaved icons of famous rappers. Cardinal and co were very impressed, but

I loathed it and took to wearing some bonnets I'd tucked in my bag during a wonderful backstage tour at Stratford (that I didn't know we weren't allowed to take). Luckily Mark repaired my botched barnet on my return to London, and created the height I like at the back with his clever cotton wool padding, which gives me a terrific turret and unlimited confidence!

So there we, are ladies, you've got long lush hair, big boobs, a bald vulva, a smooth botty two and big talony nails! Bingo! But, we have one final word of warning!

PERIODS

A big NO NO for a lady and a guaranteed way to turn off any self-respecting guy is him EVER having to experience the ghastly whiff of a lass 'with the painters in' – whether it's the browner waft of some old menstrual leftovers, or the violent meat honks of a gal at the crest of her crimson tide. Of course there are rare cases where a man enjoys a bleeding lady and wants to wag his willy in her vaginal bolognaise, but they tend to be mentally ill or living on a barge (often both). So what can we do if the rightly named 'curse' threatens to throw cold water over a fella's desire? You need The Menohoove:

THE MENOHOOVE

For big-hipped ladies with a hefty monthly flow, the Menohoove is a pretty, mini vaginal hoover that sucks out your entire menstrual contents for the month so you can enjoy yourself whatever the occasion! Maybe it's your wedding day and you're about to say 'I do' when you feel that telltale dribble in your gusset. Don't force your groom to say 'I don't' because of the big nasty red stain on your bridal gown!

Your tubby boss passes your desk and winks. You know this means it's time for some forbidden cupboard intercourse but your pants are telling a different story. With your sexy Menohoove hanging by its pearly chain off your handbag, you can simply slip to the ladies and hoover out your innards, making you fresh below so your boss can pound away to his heart's content.

Don't let your period deprive you of marriage or a promotion! Try Menohoove today.

'Cheer up your menfolk with the **MENOHOOVE**. **Swipe right** with your monthly discharge and **swipe left** for blodge-free intercourse.'

Warning, the Menohoove may cause irreparable internal damage.

So there we have it, ladies! It's time for you to get out there and nab yourself an actual hubby!

Chapter 2

WHY HE PUMPS THEN DUMPS

Getting A Ring On That Desperate Finger

As many of you will know, we've had eight husbands between us, so we certainly know a thing or two about getting a guy down the aisle! But how do we do it? Well, as fully trained Flirtologists both being fluent in the secret language of love, we have helped countless lonely celebrities, and since we are asked time and again by folk right across the globe, 'Please Joan! Please, Jericha! How do I flirt?', we thought it was about time we spilt the sex beans.

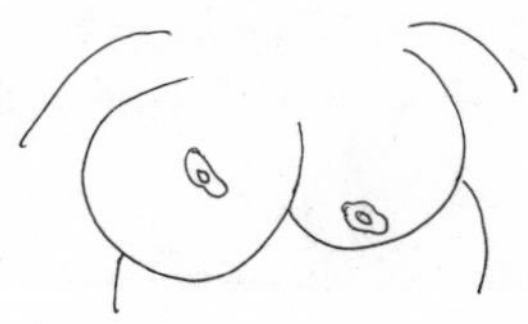

JERICHA

Yes, well my first marriage, as you know. Joan, was arranged by Mother, to a much older gentleman called Randy (I was fifteen, he seventy-one), and his idea of flirting was taking out his dentures and chomping at my crotch through my jeans until he did a dribble into his pyjamas.

JOAN

Sweet! And since then, you've had what I think is the perfect marriage with Phillip!

JERICHA

Bless you, Joan, I am lucky. Of course, as a tireless scout leader in Thailand, he does spend 98 per cent of the year away, tending to these young boys.

JOAN

But when he comes home for those couple of days it must be so charged?

JERICHA

It's electric, and he'll always bring me a gift – some big men's socks or a snack from the plane. He does unfortunately return with these nasty cold infections, but, as he has explained, they don't get colds over there like we do, it's more a type of a penis cold. But he'll still Skype the boys each evening, and if I walk by his office door, there he is, with his poor willy sneezing away.

JOAN

Bless him. And of course I'm on to hubby number six, managing Ralph in his 'turtle coma' – because he goes in and out of it – but having lost three of my guys to suicide, I'm hopeful that once Ralph 'goes', hubby number seven will finally be 'the one'!

JERICHA

Oh, I've no doubt about that, Joan! So to get back to all our dear readers – how do we flirt?

JOAN

Well, of course there's all the tried and tested methods – lots of eye contact and twirling your hair, and that actually goes for both sexes, doesn't it?

JERICHA

Yes! Nothing sexier than a guy playing around with his hair, perhaps tugging away at a few lone strands if he's balding.

JOAN

And should he mix the hair tugs with some eye contact?

JERICHA

Yes, nice big staring eyes, please. No blinking.

JOAN

Oh, I love guys who don't blink. And there are men who can actually bring a woman to climax with their eyes alone, aren't there?

JERICHA

Absolutely: Omar Sharif, Jeremy Irons …

JOAN

James Galway, the flautist, with his quickly quivering eyes.

JERICHA

Goodness, yes, all the women and many of the gay men in the audience at his concerts would spontaneously orgasm, just through watching James's flicky eyes.

JOAN

His flute obviously had an impact, but his vibrating eyes were key, so do men need to be able to do something fancy with the eyes if possible, perhaps going cross-eyed?

JERICHA

Cross-eyed is very sexy on a guy, but he'll need to keep those crossed eyes trained on our lady's boobs.

JOAN

Can he drag them up to the face occasionally?

JERICHA

Momentarily, Joan, yes, or swoop them swiftly down to the vagina, but then straight back up to the boobs, please, guys! And that should bring her to climax pretty quickly in a wine bar, particularly with those swivel stools.

JOAN

And what about touching? When should a guy touch a gal? Say, you're on the first date, you're at a restaurant.

JERICHA

Well, guys need to cut to the chase, so don't waste time touching her hand or arm.

JOAN

Go in for the boob?

JERICHA

Go in for the boob, Joan, if you grab at her boob or pummel her vulva she knows something's going on.

JOAN

So is that reaching across the table as you're having the starter?

JERICHA

Exactly. And he can do some light punching motions too, grappling, grasping, pulling, tugging.

JOAN

And this is with the vulva?

JERICHA

Yes, or the boob, or both, punch and pummel between the two.

JOAN

OK, and what about the lady here? Should she reciprocate by snatching at his penis?

JERICHA

Now be careful here, Joan. Just because he's grabbed and punched your boob or had a good old yank on your vulva doesn't mean he wants that in return. He may want a calm little gentle enfoldment of his penis.

JOAN

OK, with a wee napkin?

JERICHA

Yes, or a hanky, a lacy lady's hanky, so if you just pop it in your palm and gently fold it around the member on the outside of his trousers, sometimes guys just want that tenderness.

JOAN

Now, erogenous zones ... obviously these are different in men and women – but for guys we know it's the anus.

JERICHA

Every time, so you need to get to that, and sharpish! Now if he's sitting down, that's harder to approach.

JOAN

Well, if you go to an Asian restaurant where you've got chopsticks, you could always slide the chopsticks under the table and poke away at his anus with those?

JERICHA

Start gently, though, see how he responds. If he gives an indication that he wants something very rough, ask the waiter for a big handful of chopsticks and you can go at your date quite roughly under the table, or hand them to him and he can go roughly at you instead if that's what he likes. He might well want to have a quick prod of your nipples and boobs with them too.

Shout Out To All The Sexy Guys

Fat, thin, bald, furry, violent or very, very short: GUYS! WE WANT YOU!!! We both adored the look of men in the seventies, with their hot furry chests and gorgeous medallions. And, boy, did they know how to loosen a lady's pants with a chat-up line! With that bright shiny coin affair necklace nestling between some pink, hair-ringed nipples and the shirt unbuttoned right the way down to a big groinal fringe, they had us dangling like panting puppets on their proverbial strings. We often wonder why that truly manly look fell out of fashion!

That said, we're all over the 'anything goes' look that guys sport nowadays. You can wear what you like, when you like. Be that some snug, crotch-bulking jeans for stumpy-legged guys, some puffy dad chinos for the plumper mister, or simply fun, bright red dungarees and a big clumpy clog, we'll always want to climb aboard that love-buffet and tuck into some hot willy soup!

Another huge turn-on for us ladies is a really heavy aftershave that catches in the back of the throat. We know guys worry nowadays that their natural man-scent won't be smelt beneath it, but when you spray it on, it actually stirs up the natural activity of your pheromones and releases great puffy waves of your very own sex pong into the ether. It can even behave as a sort of aphrodisiac for the man himself, turning him on again and again as he goes about his day, popping in and out of hardware stores and greasy spoon cafes.

On a side note many guys ask us, 'Should I spray my penis with floral products to make it more palatable?' The answer is a resounding NO! There's nothing nicer than the natural smell of a ripe male penis. In short, guys, you don't need to be disguising the sort of tangy, eggy, oaky, fishy, cheddary pong coming off your frontage: we ladies love it! Indeed, there are many aftershaves that seek to mimic those aromas. Whether it's the musty overtones of an older grandad-type penis, or the fresher more 'seaside-y day out' smell of a younger man's rock-hard member, we can't get enough of your wily willy whiffs. So what are you waiting for, ladies? LET'S GET IT ON!

'I'VE GOT A DATE! BUT WHAT SHOULD I TALK ABOUT?'

Ladies, please! For goodness sake don't talk at all! He doesn't want to hear anything you have to say, he just wants a jolly good uninterrupted gawp at the goods you have on offer – and if there's any talking to be done, let *him* do it. If you do need to make a sound, let it be laughter. Often, ladies are not sure when a man's told a joke, so simply pepper the date with laughing every ten seconds or so and it's likely to coincide at least once. Laughing mimics orgasm; at first the head is cocked but coy, and then thrown back in this abandoned mouth-yapping ecstasy. It's a big aphrodisiac, causing a nice release for the lady in the groinal area, often with a little spurt into the pants, priming the body for the penis to enter.

But, ladies, you really only have one job on this date: look like a trillion zillion dollars! Be sure to have everything out on show: half a nipple, a hefty dose of bare, toned upper thigh and a clingy skirt that shows off all the contours of your vulva. But make sure any displaying of the wares looks accidental. We don't want him thinking, Oh lord, here's another easy Liz who's clearly going to flare it all open and gobble me sideways at the end of the night. That's a road to ruin and he won't be coming back for more. At this stage you want to be lighting the blue touchpaper for this fella and standing back, leaving him sleepless with engorgement after the date and beyond.

'WHAT SHOULD I EAT ON THE DATE?'

Ladies, please! Don't eat anything! Just order a banana or a plate of strawberries and get your lips around them, in between listening, looking and laughing. Or try mock fellating a breadstick. But be warned, these can snap suddenly, leaving you with crumby, gunky lips and him with a profound fear of losing his penis. If there are big chunky parmesan breadsticks available on the table, then do some sexy manoeuvring with those around your mouth, or use it to intercourse your own nostril, but watch out for unsightly paste collecting on the teeth and pongy parmesan breath travelling across the table towards him in the busy restaurant.

For added fun, you could pop some food colouring on your tongue before the date, so in a darkened wine bar he can get a good idea of its size and length, then he can picture it maypoling around his penis later. It's wise to use a luminous paint in a tangy orange or a violent pink so it really pops, but no blues or blacks please, ladies, or he'll think you're having a stroke.

'I'VE HEARD GUYS LOVE TO FEEL FAT, FULL'N' FARTY AFTER A MEAL. HOW DO I MAKE SURE HE'S SATISFIED?'

Make sure your date eats as much as possible to give him a big, fat sleepy tum and encourage him to drink plenty, which will lower his standards and give him ye olde 'beer goggles'! You can order a lasagne at the start, but ask for a banana on the side and then when the food arrives you just push your lasagne towards him with a Lady Di smile. If he's a gent he might say, 'No, that's yours', but don't take no for an answer. Make sure he gets that down him, as well as his giant steak and chunky frites. In fact, you can even feed him. Shovel the lasagne into his mouth, but make it sexy. Give him a mouthful to chew on, whilst unpeeling your banana and start pushing that in and out of your mouth, making deep grunting sounds with each banana-thrust. This is like a pornographic mouth ballet, so ideally there should be appropriate music to accompany your grunty moves. Italian restaurants are good for arias and soaring strings, so do liaise with the manager for specific pieces to be played. Failing that, bring your own mini-speaker. But avoid things that are too upbeat like 'Agadoo', or too depressing like Tracy Chapman. And do clap along if the song warrants it and he'll see a fun lady who could be marriage material!

YOUR BIG SPOON

One great tip is to always take your own big spoon with you on a date – wooden is best – so that you can reach across during the meal to get a really big dollop of whatever into his mouth. If he's already ordered a steak and seems confused by the lasagne, you need to divert him by creating an assault on all his senses. Start by jiggling your boobs and with your feet under the table, begin drumming his penis with your toes (pounding penis drumming is very sexy for a guy). And why not thump the bottom of his chair repeatedly with your shoe so it vibrates to give him a nice bottomy back thrill as well. But do practice all this at home first, because shovelling in the big spoon, grunting, clapping, fellating a bread stick, toe-drumming his penis, jiggling your boobs and kicking his chair can be a bit of a handful. It's a bit like rubbing your head and patting your tummy!

'SHOULD I AGREE TO SEX ON A FIRST DATE?'

For goodness sake DON'T offer sex on the first date unless he downright demands it. It will come across as nasty, desperate and whorey. A bit of fellating in the restaurant toilets is always fine, just don't go home with him, pull down your pants the minute you're through the door and say 'do it to me'. He may well agree to a burpy bonk, but trust us, you'll never see him again.

You do get these daft women who go in for 'coffee', say they're popping to the bathroom to 'freshen up' and before you know it, bored of waiting, he nips in to dump his whopping pre-sex stool, only to find she's laying out her overnight bag, with her heavy anti-ageing creams and morning shower cap, not to mention her KY lubricating gel and myriad contraceptives! What a turn-off! Yes, we all enjoy wearing femidoms for a bit of fun. And, yes, there are more life-threatening STDs about than ever before. But, ladies, please! DON'T push your contraception in his face. It's lovely for him that he can bareback ride, up the front and in the back, to his heart's content without thought or care. So no contraception on a first date please, or you'll blow your potential marriage gasket sky-high.

'SHOULD I COOK FOR HIM AT HOME?'

It's a risky one this, especially if you live in a studio flat where he'll be all too aware that your sofa flips into a double bed in an instant. So don't be surprised if he sees this as an invitation to pounce and penetrate. But if you live in a tidy shared house with a couple of girlfriends, make sure they're uglier than you and don nothing but a sexy apron to dazzle him with your much-hotter-than-your-ugly-friends bod and super culinary skills!

Flirty recipes to get him in the mood

JOAN'S NAUGHTY BURGERS

Ralph and I first bonded over our love of cattle, and though he's a slight man, he had what they call 'big dick energy' – even though his penis was a shocking disappointment when I first rummaged in his boxers. Like most men, Ralph always enjoyed meat and, before his coma, would wolf around ten pounds a day: four chickens for breakfast and a chain of sausages over his lunch hour. (Even now I'll get Gyulchay,* my tarty home help, to whizz him up some old bits of bone and scrag ends, and funnel them into his mouth-pipe to keep up his strength.) I gifted Ralph m'naughty burgers on our second date. We ate them wedged inside two fat, crusty baps, slathered in a stinky mayo with a basket of double-length fries and made love on the table until Ralph needed to pass a stool.

INGREDIENTS

You'll need:
A spoonful of bull beef
A big sloppy dollop of fudge ice cream
2 thrush eggs
An elderly onion
A mug of old chip oil

---

* See Appendix B.

METHOD

Bash the bull beef into a mini ball pan (Selfridges do a fab one in honeypeach for £399), and use your middle fingers to push in and out of the meat mess as if ringing a doorbell. Put on a high heat and start frying.

Place the onion in a sock (ideally of the 'pop' variety) and swing it around the kitchen, allowing it to make contact with as many surfaces as possible, before introducing it to the meat and walloping the onion mush. (Don't worry about pop-sock bits, it gives the burger a naughty, nutty texture.)

Plop your sloppy fudge dollop of ice cream and eggs into a pretty tumbler and dribble them out onto the bull mess, massaging the lot into sexy burger shapes.

Flash fry and serve with a dirty smile, in a French girl's basket bulging with steaming crusty baps.

'COFFEE?' OR 'WHEN SHOULD I FIRST INTERCOURSE?'

It's perhaps your third date, you've had a fab evening and he asks you in for 'coffee' at his place. You know this means intercourse.

You're on his couch, fooling around, and he starts nudging his penis round the back and you can feel the familiar budge of your own queuing faeces. So now is the time to say you want to 'freshen up' and hotfoot it to his bathroom with a vital item you'll have tucked into your handbag 'just in case': your Pumpapoo.

THE PUMPAPOO!

Pumpapoo is a quick and fun way to clear your bowels before a sexy session, much like an enema, but without all the brown slosh.

Pumpapoo shoots up a yummy jelly, in **Naughty Raspberry, Tarty Tangerine** or **Lusty Lemon**, which binds everything together so the Pumpa vacuum can suck out a full-length brown snake (usually around 2 metres long) that can coil perfectly into the Pumpapoo canister.*

PUMPAPOO comes in 5 different handy sizes!

---

* Do remember you are doing this in your boyfriend's bathroom, so be sure to seal up the Pumpapoo canister so he doesn't find your giant poo snake in the morning!

So now you're good to go and ready to do the dirty deed. But remember this is about your guy getting pleasure, so for goodness sake don't start griping about the F-word ... FOREPLAY!

JOAN

We get a lot of ladies moaning that their guy doesn't believe in foreplay and then when he goes to insert his penis it's too dry.

JERICHA

I could knock these women's heads together, Joan! Guys don't have time for foreplay.

JOAN

Could it be that he wants it to be dry?

JERICHA

Well, yes, there is this new trend for that, because he's desperate for a bit of friction ...

JOAN

Yes. So this used to be what we called 'dry humping', basically teenagers in jeans bumping uglies, getting all soggy and young willies getting torn to shreds on the zip, but now there's this trend for actual dry sex?

JERICHA

Indeed. Dry and even dusty sex has become a must-have, because a lot of ladies have been enjoying themselves too much and getting moist to the point of flooding. So the poor guy is getting lost in this big sloppy receptacle.

JOAN

And a very small penis will just come flying out?

JERICHA

Flying out, Joan, which is no fun for
him. But you'd be surprised how many
women are overreacting this way and
producing ghastly amounts of vaginal mucus.

JOAN

And to be clear it actually is mucus,
just as you'd have in the nose?

JERICHA

Exactly the same, Joan, as when you have
a very heavy cold.

JOAN

And can you get vaginal bogies?

JERICHA

The vagina is packed with bogies, Joan,
which is why you so often see ladies
picking at their pants in Sainsbury's.

JOAN

Can you blow the vagina before intercourse, as
you would blow your nose?

JERICHA

Yes, you can, and you should. But be
careful not to go at it too much, as
you may tear off a portion.

JOAN

And you'd just use a normal tissue?

JERICHA
I think it's nice to make it part of the
lovemaking session, so make sure to have a
pretty hankie and sex it up with some lace.

JOAN
Could you blow your vagina in front of
your guy?

JERICHA
You can make it a part of your
seduction routine, yes.

JOAN
And does the vagina ever sneeze?

JERICHA
More often than you'd think Joan. It
also snores at night, which most
ladies are not aware of, but this
could well be contributing to your
fella's building lack of desire and the potential
loss of a marriage proposal.

WHO IS RESPONSIBLE FOR CONTRACEPTION?

As we all know, contraception is a woman's department, so for goodness sake, don't expect these poor guys to suffocate their penis in a thick rubber sheath. Men simply don't have time to go and buy condoms or order them online and if you provide one and expect him to force it onto his thickened pipe mid-pump, you may as well just punch him in the face.

Obviously there can be extreme situations when a condom can be used. And thank goodness, girls are taught sexy ways to put one on a guy in school nowadays, using just her mouth, whilst simultaneously fingering his anus. Mum (or Gran if she lives in) can also show daughters how to do this, using a banana and a Hula Hoop, as part of her general homemaking education. And it can be lovely for Gran to get her gummy mouth around an old banana and nod her shrivelled neck up and down to remind her of her fellatio years.

But condoms are only to be used in extreme cases. For example, if he has a very infected, disintegrating penis or a chronic STD. He will rightly still want intercourse, but the condom in this scenario is practical, holding his penis together to stop it collapsing inside the lady's vagina.

It's also very nasty for a lady to ask a gentleman to withdraw his penis before ejaculation (unless she's going to gulp down his sex glue). Making him 'pull out' and then weep his white glory onto some old bed sheets or a cellulitey thigh, is akin to stealing a baby from a cot. Yes, some gentleman enjoy painting a lady's boobs with his baby-batter, but mostly they want to stay inside the lady and fart themselves to sleep.

Both of us have found a fab thing to do to help guys out, which is to pop a femidom in before a night out – even if it's a night out with the girls, you never know, you might get lucky! If you get into the habit, it's as easy as brushing your teeth. They are big and noisy so if he mentions the crackling sound, just say it must be his tinnitus – and yes, they do have a tendency to fall out and you may find yourself having dinner in a smart restaurant, getting up to go to the ladies, only to have it plop out at your feet. But the good news is you'll get very adept at distracting your guy by jiggling your boobs or somesuch, whilst quietly scooping your 'dom up and popping it back in as you make your way between the tables. Be sure to carry a pair of Jericha's 'FemiTongs' in your handbag at all times to scoop with ease!

Some guys say a lady wearing a femidom is like having sex with a plastic bag, in which case the lady should be on the Pill, or get a coil fitted. The really big, painful ones work best so do pop down to your GP.

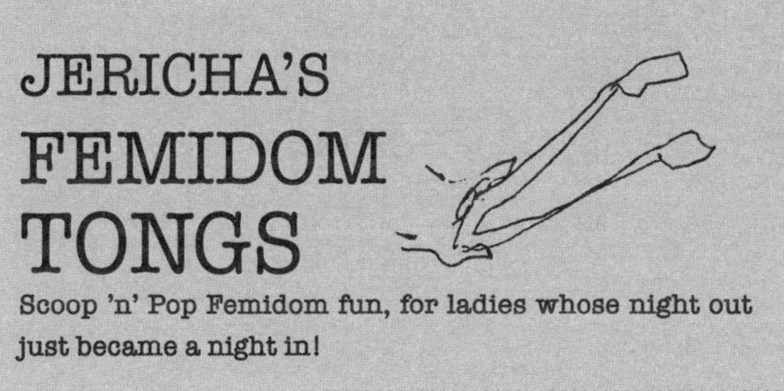

JERICHA'S
FEMIDOM
TONGS
Scoop 'n' Pop Femidom fun, for ladies whose night out just became a night in!

'HOW MANY SEXUAL POSITIONS SHOULD I OFFER HIM?'

We're asked time and again about what sexual positions we should be doing and how many per session. For a woman it's between twelve and twenty per session. For men they really don't have time to think about these things, and why should they?

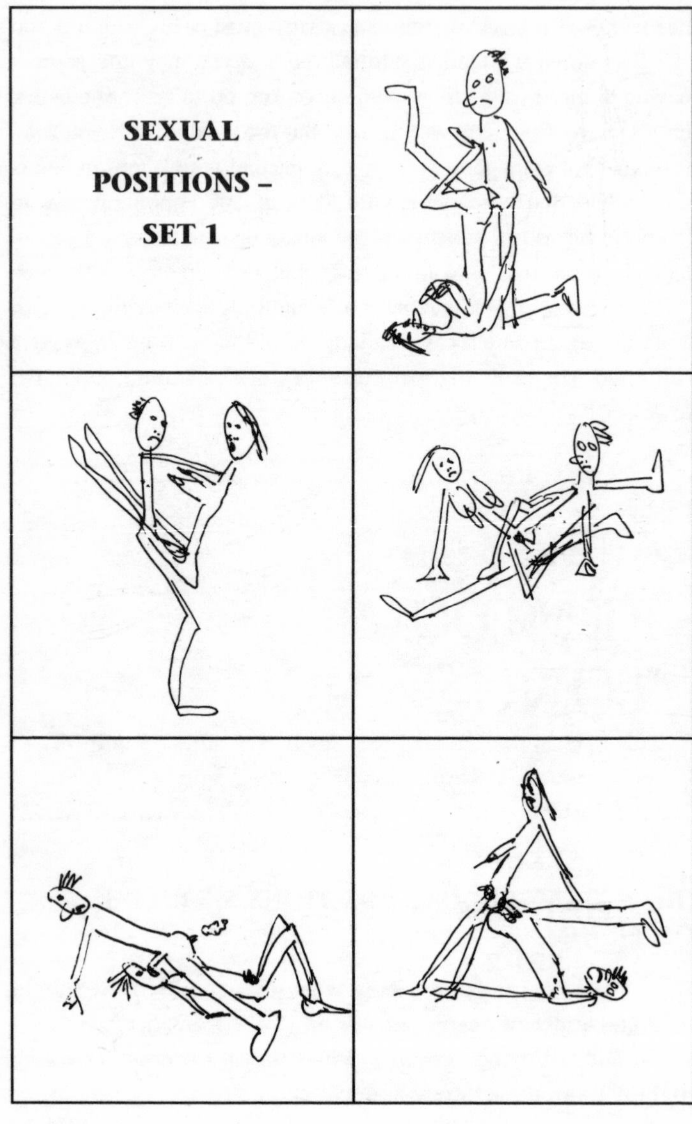
SEXUAL
POSITIONS –
SET 1

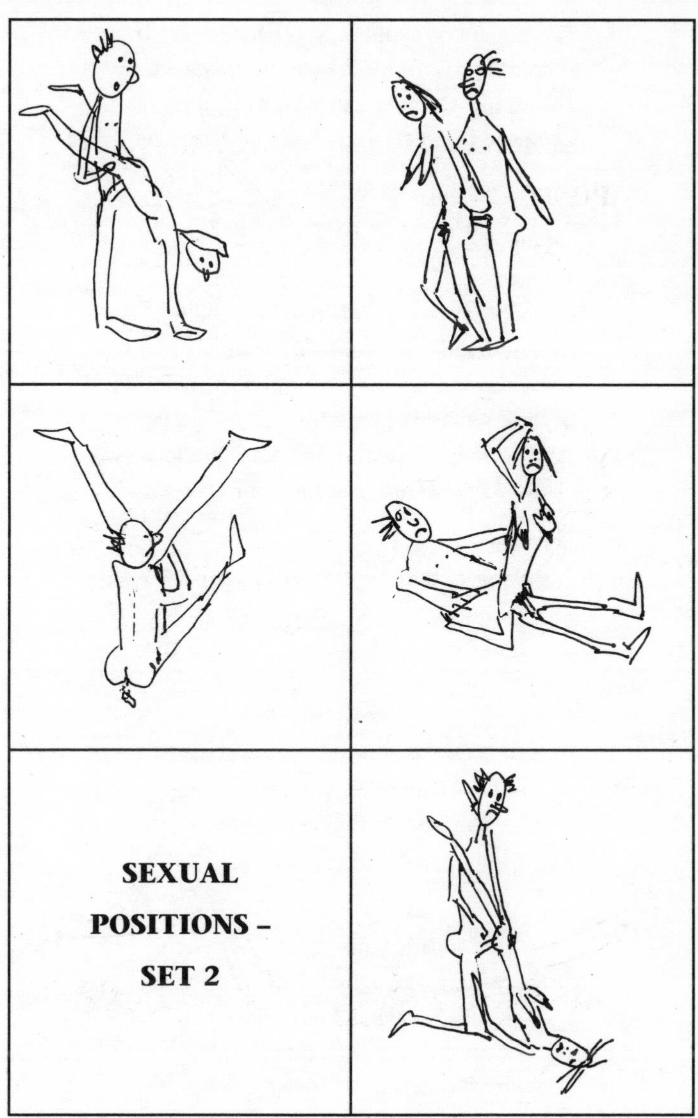
SEXUAL
POSITIONS –
SET 2

JOAN

To get a guy to propose, you need to be a bit different and offer more bangs for his buck. So things like sex press-ups whilst clapping his penis in between sucks is very impressive.

JERICHA

So how does this work exactly?

JOAN

So your guy is lying flat, and you're on top, hands either side of his thighs like a lizard, and you're doing your press-ups, and in between you're clapping the sides of his penis and sucking on it, and then you should go into a handstand, and flip yourself over.

JERICHA

So you've doubled back over yourself?

JOAN

Yes.

JERICHA

And then flip yourself back over again to land fair and square, with either the anus or vagina onto his upstanding penis?

JOAN

Ideally you want to be alternating – a vaginal bounce, an anal bounce, a vaginal bounce, an anal bounce, and twist, and twist, and twist until bingo! He ejaculates.

JERICHA
Wonderful.

JOAN
In the early days of Ralph and myself, I'd often do a naked handstand against the wall in the corner whilst Ralph would be busy doing some DIY – then he'd notice me and come on over for a little chomp in between jobs.

JERICHA
But I know you'd be there for quite a while sometimes, before he'd notice?

JOAN
Yes! And often faint through all the blood to my head. Not only that but Ralph being so slight, and already bent sideways with an arthritic spine, he wasn't up to much. Plus he had that tiny parroty tongue and small tight mouth, so he never satisfied me in that way down there.

JERICHA
Awful, Joan.

LADY-CUM-KWIK

It's very upsetting for a guy to feel that although he's been jabbing away somewhere in the region of your clitoral nub for one or two minutes, you still haven't orgasmed.

Well, fear not! Help is at hand with our new LADY-CUM-KWIK. Simply clip your feet into the electronic pads at the base of the machine and the corkscrew action will swivel you hither and thither to simulate ecstatic writhing. Then when the time feels right simply press the maximum-judder button to shake your body frantically and make you appear to be orgasming. All you need to do is make the appropriate noises and he'll be in heaven.

Remember he's unlikely to look at your face, but in case he does, he doesn't want to witness the ghastly sight of a grin-faced harridan having fun, so do practice some sexy 70s porn faces. Or ideally don a printed mask of his celebrity crush.

Yummy Nosh So Your Guy Can Go Again!

Guys get really sleepy after copulating, or even watching you have a fake orgasm on a machine. So why not whip him up this protein-rich yummy snack whilst he's snoozing, so that he's revived and ready for you to hop back on board and ride his dicky 'til dawn!

MAHMOUD'S EGGY BULBS

Mahmoud loves to cook these tasty eggy bulbs when he gets home, after a hard day of hysterectomies (often performing up to thirty-five a day!). He needs the egg to replenish his semen (he sometimes leaks a touch of ejaculate when operating), and plopping his long olivey fingers in yolk and flour, with some Chopin tinkling on his iPod, is very soothing after a day of wrestling wombs.

He always adds a touch of harissa to the mix, a wonderfully pungent paste that builds big fat sperms and is also a favourite sexy base note in many of Mahmoud's highly seductive man-perfumes. It was his mother who first taught the young chap (a round and jolly little fellow) how to make these energising snacks. Fatima would roll the eggy paste into these pretty bulbs, often placing them near her boobs in jest, to the glorious ring of Mahmoud's childish giggles, then smear on the harissa and finish things off with just a dribble of her middle-aged spittle.

INGREDIENTS

You'll need:
3 eggs on the turn
Some Indian sugar
A smudge of harissa
Unsalted butter
Plain flour
Cornflakes
Fatima's spittle or similar. Female spittle is best, but be wary of old people's as it contains mostly mould.

METHOD

Pop on some luxury loungewear and Classic FM and get your eggs, butter, sugar and flour into a large ramekin and fondle into little bulb shapes, smear on the harissa gently (as if tending to some chafed testes) and bounce the bulb on a bed of cornflakes until it's nicely covered, dribble some spittle (don't worry about brushing your teeth first) across the entire collection and pop in the oven on a high heat for ten minutes until your bulbs are crusty.

Serve with a small glass of sherry and some oak-smoked peanuts.

Love Horoscopes

We all love a bit of science behind our relationships and the Joan and Jericha LOVEMATCH blood tests are now available at £2,500 each, meaning we can join perfect couples together via their blood types. But for those of you more mystically inclined (and with less wonga to splash), let's look to the stars for inspiration:

VIRGO WOMAN AND TAURUS MAN

VIRGO:
These women tend to wear mostly navy and are somewhat spindly and angular to look at, with angry nipples and rather large lower halves. They generally have tubby pudendas, which can get pongy if housed in tights all day. These are anxious, serious ladies and the bowel is very much the Virgo's Achilles heel, which often leads to bouts of the runs or hours straining on the loo. They are usually bitter, judgemental spinsters and often suited to a life based around the church. But if they wed, they are surprisingly agile in the bedroom.

TAURUS:
Perfectly suited to a Virgo, these guys are built to last. Big bovine fellas with fat, sausagey fingers and thick, juicy willies, the Taurean man just loves to hump away at you any which way he can, as long as you give him a nice bacon sandwich after. He will need intercourse at least twice a day and loves you bouncing away on his plump prick, as long as the sheets are made of silk! The bull loves to get his big tongue in and pleasure his lady's front bottom, but don't ask for anything subtle as he prefers a lick, a burp and a 'Where's my bacon sandwich?' He enjoys being teased and tickled so do be sure to fiddle with his anus wherever possible, especially if you're making him watch a box set like *The Crown*.

LEO LADY AND ARIES GUY

LEO:
The lumpy lioness. These ladies are big spoilt show-offs. Wide, dimply and prone to hefty periods and pebbly stools, the Leo lass loves to lollop and expects you to bring her snacks and treats whilst she lounges in front of the TV. Mostly unemployed, these women fly into rages if provoked, so any man willing to take one on has his work cut out.

ARIES:
The rampant ram. These are guys that want to fuck. They like strong, toned women, with big boobs and tight bubble butts, although will take on a Leo lass for a lost weekend. But please, no tears, ladies. These lads will not tolerate a weepy lass. They like ballsy buxom girls who tell it like it is and smack them round the face when they're out of line. Slapping, kicking, punching, strangling, these are like catnip to the Aries man. He loves rough foreplay and can often be found headbutting his partner whilst she sleeps. Naughty old ram!

PISCES LASS AND GEMINI FELLA

PISCES:

Long, lank ladies, make no mistake: these women do smell. The face tends to look quite morose with droopy, cloudy eyes and wet floppy lips. These are slippery customers, always changing her tune and turning up late for appointments. More often than not this woman will be a dental assistant who likes to watch reality TV and is most likely fellating her boss (the hunky sixty-something dentist who just got back from skiing and a cheeky facelift). She loves to slither about the place, flirting with every Tom, Dick and Harry, so don't invite her over for dinner if you want to hold on to hubby!

GEMINI:

The flighty twins. These guys tend to be light, wiry and super flirty – think Michael Douglas in his heyday. Twinkly, hot eyes, a chunky penis and thin, high hair – and, boy, do these guys know how to dress! Sexy linen suits, sockless loafers and no underwear. Ever. You will have to put up with some nasty dark moods from the evil twin, sulky huffs and toxic botty puffs if you look at him the wrong way, but make him a fishy soup with a glass of champers and he'll be back to normal. The nice twin is clown-funny and an acrobat between the sheets, which is why he just can't be faithful.

LIBRAN LOVELY AND SAGITTARIUS GENT

LIBRA:

These women are dull as dishwater, but with killer bods. They often have plain repetitive faces, but guys love that and he's not going to be looking at your face that often anyway.

SAGITTARIUS:

These guys have curly hair, smiley eyes and cute button noses, which can be a turn-off as most ladies love big angry hooters. Sagman is the archer, so he's one of life's go-getters and tends to have a penis shaped like an arrow which can be a lot of fun and suits the Libran lady's long vaginal vestibule, which is usually shaped like a Toblerone.

SCORPIO GAL AND CAPRICORN MAN

SCORPIO:
Bitch on wheels, these are roly-poly ladies who are dynamite between the sheets and able to fellate up to six guys in one sitting. But life with a Scorpio lass is no picnic (though she'll always want one), weeping one minute and puncturing your thigh with a knife the next. Most of these types will end up in prison humping anything that moves, and are likely to be frequent visitors to A&E with rodents and larger wildlife crammed up their front botties.

CAPRICORN:
These wily goats are tough as nails, which is how they can handle that vicious Scorpio sting. They'll build you a house, but don't expect him to be in it: he'll be too busy scaling mountains. But when this gorgeous goat gets home, he'll need you to tend to his horny hooves and siphon off some sex cheese. He's actually very frightened of his Scorpio lady which is why he goes on so many trips and often ends up kissing a man he's met up a mountain.

CANCER MISS AND AQUARIAN MISTER

CANCER:
The homely crab, these ladies tend to be stumpy, short-legged lasses who waddle about with a worried ruddy complexion and rather piggened eyes. You'll generally find them in a dead-end job, frequently an underground office, loitering by the water cooler

hoping to nab a mate. They don't mind tubby guys as long as he goes on top, though the crab will enjoy the occasional doggy or sideways cowgirl, if she's had plenty of Prosecco. Birthing is very tricky for the crab lady, as not only do they suffer with Vaginisimisimus (which is double vaginismus and will lock and strangle the penis for up to three hours once inside the vaginal vestibule), but they are prone to locked uterus, making labour impossible. There have even been cases where the baby has had to be delivered out of the lady's side.

AQUARIUS:
Moody, moody, moody! Watch out for these guys. Often magicians both literally and figuratively, they always masturbate in leather gloves and tend to go bald the moment you marry them.

Marriage

So there we are. You've learnt everything you need to know to enable you to secure yourself an engagement from someone and that's the key here. Don't be too fussy, ladies! People these days want far too much from a marriage: 'Oh, I want someone nice-looking, who I get on with', but where does that leave the rest of us? It's not a shopping list, ladies! That said we both wrote our top three:

JOAN
Mine was looks, money and penis size. I was sick of these tiny penises, but ironically ended up with Ralph who had not just the tiny penis and a parrot-y tongue, but an actual underlying condition called Alice in Wonderland disease, where elements of the body, often the genitals, shrink dramatically. Combine that with his enlarged heart issues and galloping arthritis, and I honestly can't believe what I've been through! But I'm gagging for hubby number

seven who's gonna be rich and gorgeous with a giant penis. I just have to wait for Ralph to pass away.

JERICHA

Well, my three were suave, attentive and, crucially of course, sporty. I'm substantially bigger than Phillip as you know, Joan, and as a strong butterfly swimmer from the age of twelve I did develop huge shoulders that many people thought were padded, so I wore lots of capes, which thankfully were pretty fashionable at the time. It did seem to scare a lot of the guys off, thinking I was some kind of witch or an actress, but eventually I found dear Phillip – and what a wonderful match that has turned out to be, as you say. I'm very blessed.

Chapter 3

WHY HE NEEDS TO PORK OTHER LADIES WHEN YOU'RE PREGNANT

Getting Your Baby Daddy's Needs Met

The wedding itself should be a wonderful time for all the guys to have fun. The groom can look forward to some dirty anal with a few of the bridesmaids in one of the big disabled toilets, and elderly male relatives or lonely local men who may have put money towards the bride's surgical enhancements can now, quite rightly, ask for some return on their investments. Often they'll be happy with a simple honk on your hooters, so do get into the spirit please, ladies!

Please don't expect your wedding night to be like something from the movies. Your husband has seen it all before and will be exhausted from porking all the boozy bridesmaids. You've no doubt been a veritable Bridezilla from the moment you got that ring on your grasping little finger, so now's the time to step back and let hubby enjoy his wedding night with a much-deserved snory sleep in the lush four-poster whilst you bed down in the en-suite bath. It's worth giving your vagina the night off anyway, as you'll have chronic cystitis throughout your honeymoon due to hubby's increased demands for anal (no doubt fantasising about his filthy frolics with the buxom bridesmaids), so your urethra will be inundated with faecal bits as he swipes his willy about front and back in a double-hole frenzy. And you'll likely end up with some bridesmaid-based herpes too.

On your honeymoon, do be prepared to see hubby's eyes start wandering. With too much time on his hands, he'll start to feel the cold dread of the life ahead of him, seeing you boiled red from sunburn and rather porkier than your pre-wedding, starvation-diet bod. You'll need to cut him some slack if he leaves you to sunbathe solo whilst he has a cuddle or two with some hot totty on the beach, even if that cuddle involves his penis.

Welcome to married bliss! Your only job now is to make sure to conceive, and quickly, ideally a week after tying the knot, or he'll think he's married a dud! And don't use 'keeping your legs up to stop sperm falling out' as an excuse to skimp on the housework, we can all dust on our backs, ladies!

'I'm Pregnant!'

Congratulations! This is a wonderful moment and the fact you got pregnant means the world knows someone was prepared to have sexual intercourse with you, which makes you passably attractive and, thank goodness, married.

Sadly, you yourself will be very unattractive during this upcoming period (that said, hubby will have been going off you since the honeymoon) and though some women claim to feel 'horny' when hosting a bun in their oven, your groom will be very frightened of your big veiny hooters and dinner-plate nipples lolling atop your fat front barrel, so don't be surprised if he's off on his travels, putting it about a bit, whilst you are at your most unsightly. Don't panic, it will most likely just be with one of your close friends, or if you have a competitive mother she may see this as her chance to swoop in and ride his jiggle machine in her new M&S basque, whilst you vomit in the downstairs toilet.

Well-meaning folk speak of ladies 'blooming' during pregnancy, but beware – this can turn you into rather a tubby tart, prancing about in slutty crop tops, exposing your ghastly space hopper tum and expecting sexual interest where there simply is none. Only waxy fat men who still live with Mum and masturbate on the toilet (whilst doing a number two) actually want intercourse with a pregnant lady. These guys are medically known as *foetaphiles* and are only after one thing – nudging as close to the babe in the sac as they can with their long translucent penises. Some sexually frustrated ladies do succumb to these ghoulish guys, whilst others find solace fiddling with their nipples and nudging their mons repeatedly against tins in supermarkets, when they should be at home doing hot yoga.

In the unlikely event that hubby attempts to mount you, always stay heavily made up and be sure to get on all fours so he isn't put off by your bumpy frontage. And do be aware, baby hears and sees everything through the womb walls, including Dad's 'I'm-having-a-stroke' sex face and Mum's strangled climax cries, so do keep things pretty, ladies, please!

'IS GIVING BIRTH JUST LIKE PASSING A HUMAN STOOL?'

No, it's not. It's much worse. Many women have a profound fear of giving birth. And rightly so.

JOAN

Obviously I was able to birth all five of my
children in an exclusive private hospital with

pretty-bottomed midwives, who'd delivered
celebrity babies and many royal ones, even
those with extra heads that were promptly
carted off and locked away in the Tower.

JERICHA

Indeed, my birth with Cardinal was
rather less glamorous.
It began in a busy London airport, whilst
Phillip* was off looking for the executive
lounge, which his ticket allowed him access to.
Fortunately, there was a highly knowledgeable
male cleaner – Bejoy, who it transpired had
trained as a consultant obstetrician back in
Nigeria, but was unable to secure an equivalent
role here – and on seeing my distress rushed me
to hospital where I had to be cut bilaterally due
to the size of Cardinal's head, meaning I was
essentially flipped back like a Pez to deliver her,
which took over thirty-six hours.

Unusual and inspiring stories both. But for most women, the act of birthing will mean passing their baby in the back of a farty Uber or a friend's toilet, or at best in an NHS hospital with angry nurses shouting at them to breastfeed, as they yank their boobs and shovel them into the newborn's closed and angry mouth. This is completely normal.

And with hubby already exhausted having endured nine ghastly months of you waddling about like a puffing ape, please don't then bore him with your 'woes on the ward' should he come to visit, which he is under no obligation to do.

---

* See Appendix B.

BIRTHS FROM HELL!

Of course, there are always tales of ladies who claim they simply breathed through the birth, orgasming as baby's head finally came out, with their pasty ginger hubby rubbing away at their back and some smelly, barge-dwelling bint with hairy armpits singing out of tune and clinking some bells she found in a bin to welcome baby into the world. This is sheer nonsense and very unhygienic. The fact is most births will be horrific.

JERICHA

Yes, I have a rather unpleasant tale of a friend who had triplets, you may remember her? Angela Smithers – very haunted face and hefty behind.

JOAN

Rather a timid woman with a whiteish coating to her tongue?

JERICHA

That's her! Very difficult nose. Anyway, these triplets absolutely trashed her nethers, poor old Angela – she had to have complete vaginal restructuring surgery.

JOAN

Gosh, she had them all vaginally?

JERICHA

Yes – and all at once because they were in such a hurry to exit.

JOAN

Three at a time, rather than plopping out one b'one?

JERICHA

Exactly! It's almost as if they'd struck up a little pact in the womb and had a competition as to who could get out first. So poor old Angela was straining away and the three heads started crowning at once – and everybody panicked. Even the doctor fainted as this trio of wailing heads came bursting through.

JOAN

Gosh.

JERICHA

And then they were wedged, just howling outside Angela's vagina for about three hours as they couldn't get the shoulders through.

JOAN

Goodness, sounds like a sort of Medieval Gorgon Fest!

JERICHA

Ghastly scene, yes. Her husband filmed the whole thing which he then posted straight online, which was a terrible humiliation for everyone concerned as Angie also passed quite a hefty batch of stools. He's now left her, understandably. I mean her vagina was in absolute ribbons, Joan, ribbons!

JOAN

I can imagine there must have been almost nothing left of it?

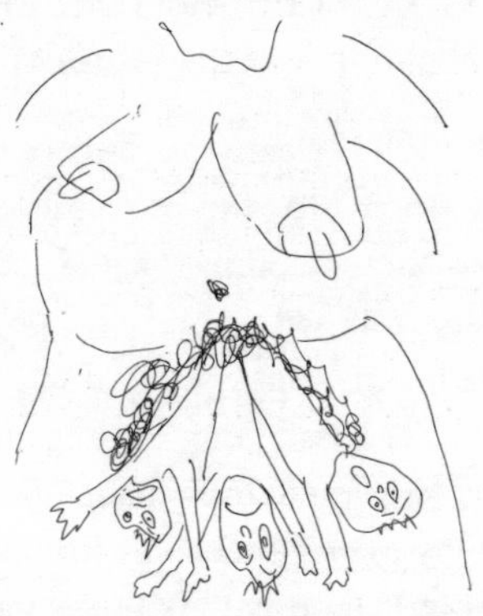

JERICHA

Nothing, I mean she basically split from hip to hip. They did their best, but it's not really worth her trying to involve herself in any intercourse now, and they had to restructure her anus, so that's now halfway up her back, poor woman.

JOAN

Goodness.

JERICHA

She has got a very close friend now, Peter, but there's nothing sexual, I think he's had all sorts of cancers that have rendered him inactive from the nipples down, really.

JOAN

But they have a wonderful companionship, I suppose?

JERICHA

Yes. Although he doesn't have long.

'SHOULD I BE SEXUALLY AVAILABLE AS SOON AS BABY IS BORN?'

Of course! The birth itself is clearly not a place for a man so please don't invite him to attend. To witness this sweaty ogress panting and grimacing atop an exploding vagina, scatter-gunning the midwives and passing folk with your anal pellets, would render most men impotent for life. But once you've passed the infant, if hubby does decide to pay a visit (and, once again, he's certainly not obliged to) do make sure you're fully made up, clad in a slutty bra and pretty thong ready to give him some furious manual, or better still oral, release behind the tiny curtain separating you from the other haggard-looking post-natal ladies. A quick and furtive willy-sneeze behind a hospital curtain will bring you closer as a couple, but do remember to pop a rag or muslin over baby's prying eyes.

Word to the wise here. Make sure to move beds if you do happen to find yourself next to a young hottie, as inevitably hubby will be too distracted by his pulsing erection to look at your mewling newborn if taut little Tara is parading her giant young boobs and unscathed vulva around the ward at visiting time. And of course it's worth mentioning here, too, that fathers aren't interested in babies or children until they're around nine or ten and ready to play violent contact sports, so please don't expect him to look at it more than once when he visits.

If it's a girl baby then obviously he won't look at all, unless you've kept the gender a secret for a grand unveiling, in which case don't be surprised if he needs to strike you repeatedly to let off some understandable steam.

'WHAT DO I DO IF I DON'T LIKE MY BABY?'

This is actually very likely, and people need to be more honest about how disappointed they often are. Obviously your first port of call is to simply swap your baby for someone else's, which is very easy as most mothers are weeping for the first few days, or hallucinating on morphine, so you can always fiddle with their pump and knock them out for an hour, whilst you do the old switcheroo.

If you've not been able to exchange your baby for a better one, then ask a lonely relative or depressed single friend if they'll take baby off you, or once you're out of hospital you can leave it on a posh-looking doorstep in the dead of night. Some ladies even pop baby in a pretty basket and shunt him up the canal. If it worked in the Bible, it can work for you!

All of these are good solid options, but if these have not been successful, you are going to be lumbered for the best part of five years, unless you can get them into boarding school earlier. Many of the better ones are now taking children at three months. These schools are pricey and often run by people who have been on some kind of register, but are well worth it, all things considered.

'IS MY BABY ATTRACTIVE?'

No. In the majority of cases the answer is in the negative, but no one will tell you that. Though hubby, if he has visited, only needs a fleeting glance at your womb offering to register that you've birthed him a monster. Mothers tend to have 'mum goggles' (a bit like beer goggles) caused by bonding hormones, which make her genuinely believe this old-man hobbit-ghoul, growling in a blanket, is somehow attractive and worth showing off.

JOAN

Very few babies are born nice-looking,
I know with Cardinal you didn't bond for—

JERICHA

It was about three years, Joan.

JOAN

And her looks have never really improved.

JERICHA

No, when she was born the consultant said her
face was like a Picasso after a stroke.

JOAN

Goodness and she's got that eye that still drifts
towards the middle and the very big head that's
not gone away ...

JERICHA

No. It's only got bigger, Joan, and as
you know she struggles for hats.

JOAN

You must have been so disappointed.

JERICHA

I think it was hard because Phillip was way
throughout those early months and unfortunately
when he did finally see her, he was physically sick.

JOAN

She was bald as well, wasn't she?

JERICHA

She had a mostly bald dome Joan, with an
old man's horseshoe of hair at the base.

JOAN

Which she had until she was fourteen?

JERICHA

Fourteen, yes, then it finally started growing, but as you know, the top was more like pubic hair.

JOAN

Ghastly yes, because really everyone just wants a pretty baby who plops out, photo ready, for you to get those images straight onto Facebook.

JERICHA

And, of course, sadly people are going to judge you on how attractive your baby is.

JOAN

Yes, ugly children can result in broken marriages, lost jobs and cancer.

JERICHA

The good news is you can actually start altering things when the baby is still in the womb, using keyhole surgery to tweak these ghastly noses or thin lips very early on – and boost baby's booty if you're wanting a Kardashian-style tot.

JOAN

And with the boy babies, they can lengthen the penis in the womb if need be?

JERICHA

Yes! They simply pipe in some 'long, chunky penis' DNA, and you can pretty well tailor the length and shape you're after. So when baby comes out, the body will have grown around this nice big penis.

JOAN

And everybody's a lot happier. You're so much prouder of your boy baby, aren't you, if he's got a lengthy member?

JERICHA

Absolutely! It means you can change him in public without worrying about people judging, saying, 'Oh dear, hasn't he got a little tiny pee pee?' Well, no, he's got a jolly good-sized pee pee, thank you very much!

JOAN

And then they get these wonderfully big erections don't they, these baby boys? So life enhancing. You see him enjoying Mum changing his nappy, looking up at her lovingly …

JERICHA

Yes, starting to create his sexual map, Joan, for the future, when he

lights on a pretty blonde in a bar.
Has she got the same eyes as Mum?

JOAN
Has she got the same glasses as Mum?

JERICHA
Does she smell like Mum?

JOAN
Do her boobs droop forward like Mum?

JERICHA
Is this lady on the bar stool going
to be wiping and tidying me down
below, like Mum?

JOAN
It's a lovely starting place for
what baby's going to find sexy now
and as he gets older.

JERICHA
And what's really nice, Joan, is that all
the other mums will gather round
and gasp at your son's penis.

JOAN
Similarly with the girl babies,
you'll want to fix up her nethers
if she's got one of these exploding
sandwiches going on downstairs.

JERICHA
Yes, these ghastly, bacony, open-Scandinavian-
style sandwich vaginas.

JOAN

Oh, I've seen many a baby girl,
pretty face and all sweet up top
but then down below there's a big
dangly clitoris and everybody's
horrified, the grandparents turn
away, the nurses make their excuses ...

JERICHA

Yes, she's there with this overripe, giant,
elongated old fig of a thing, plummeting
down to her knees. I've seen many a nurse
flee at the sight.

JOAN

So, it's best to get that keyhole-trimmed in the
womb, so she can impress uncles and aunts
alike with her pretty little hidden bell.

'MIGHT MY UGLY BABY BECOME ATTRACTIVE AT SOME POINT?'

Unlikely. If anything, it's likely to become a lot worse as the child grows and the features biggen and spread. If you have not had the foresight to have in-utero keyhole surgery, then you want to be booking baby in for 'work' as soon as you've got them home from the hospital. If surgery still isn't an option, then use heavy make-up and dark clothing to cover baby's face from prying, judgemental and horrified eyes. Hoods and hats are great, balaclavas best, if your child has a particularly difficult face. There's no two ways about it: attractive people fare better in every sphere of life. And here, as always, the outlook for boys is far rosier. A gormless-looking boy with a big hooked nose and wall eyes can be seen as fun and distinguished, whereas, quite rightly, a girl with the same features will have to become a lesbian or work in a care home for the rest of her life.

'IS MY BABY WEIRD?'

Nine times out of ten, YES, there will be something awry. Usually it's about taking drastic action, but on occasion, it may actually be something you can embrace.

JOAN
'Dear Joan and Jericha, my fiancé and I recently had a baby girl and everything was great til I got her home and realised she had boobs. I haven't told anyone else and I've been trying to massage them away but it seems to be making them bigger.' And that's from Deirdra McCroggan in Dublin.

JERICHA
So she's not just talking about these sort of spreading fatty chest buns you get in an obese infant.

JOAN
No, if you look at the picture there, Baby Clodagh has got some really rather nice developing little boobs.

JERICHA
Oh, lovely, yes, and that's a sweet little trainer bra they've popped her in for the picture.

JOAN

Yes, with a wee matching thong.

JERICHA

Very nice, this little lingerie set, and actually
the more this happens – and it is becoming
more common, babies with boobs and
little pubic tufts – the more the manufacturers
are responding. M&S, Debenhams …

JOAN

Ann Summers do a lovely baby range
of baby basques and nipple tassels.

JERICHA

Yes, and in the advert the baby is
holding a sexy rattle, tongue out …

JOAN

But I suppose with this mum being
Irish, all that Guinness has pushed
baby into puberty early.

JERICHA

Yes, and the fact is, Joan, she will have looked
super, filling out her christening gown.

JOAN

Yes, a little bit of lumping on the frontage is
lovely, isn't it. I mean, everything just looks
better with boobs doesn't it?!

JERICHA

Indeed. And all right, some
parents get upset, but others don't
mind.

JOAN

Should they consider surgery?

JERICHA

Clodagh can certainly get a breast enlargement if they feel there's not enough going on down there.

JOAN

I meant more of a boob reduction.

JERICHA

Goodness, no. No, if anything I'd say go bigger ...

JOAN

Go hard or go home!

JERICHA

Yes, and I'd be getting her to meet some boy babies on the same level physically. There's really no reason why a little baby girl can't go on a nice date with a baby boy with a smattering of pubic hair and a ready engorgement that perhaps has developed over those first few special weeks with Mum.

JOAN

And where would you suggest Clodagh and hairy Baby Donal might go on a date?

JERICHA

Obviously the cinema is great, you get these relaxed baby screenings where you can scream and do what you like. And soft play can be quite a fun, flirty atmosphere ...

JOAN
And what if they wanted something
more romantic for, say, a sexy dinner out?

JERICHA
I believe Ann Summers now have
a cafe for the littlies, one year and under,
where you can reserve a mini booth and order
the mushed-up veggies sharing platter with a
babyccino, or a naughty mocktail.

JOAN
Isn't that lovely!

Drippy Hooters

The decision to breastfeed or not is a very hot potato. Either Mum will be brandishing her big drippy hooters all round Costa, constantly swiping them over baby's screwed-up face as he's clearly trying to sleep, and then stalking off to the loo with one still dangling, frightening the elderly or trying to tempt depressed men to ditch their laptops and hop over for a grisly gobble at her ghastly guzzle pumps.

Or she'll be the angry anorexic type who's hurtling baby around the park in his souped-up Bugaboo, tossing him in the air to a chain of passers-by in order to tone her translucent stick arms, forcing him to drink a vegan-based formula, too vain to keep him alive naturally, for fear he'll tarnish her tiny taut teats.

JOAN

Some women claim they actually can't breastfeed.

JERICHA

Well that's just nonsense. That said, if you're actually not creating milk then you're simply not meant to be a mother. And incidentally, this will be apparent from an early age. Girls as young as ten should be getting tiny wet patches in their trainer bras at the sight of a hunky male model in their teen mag. If they're not, it may be a good idea to pop down to your GP.

JOAN

Absolutely, and sometimes with these dry-nippled new mums, it's just about facing the fact: 'this isn't for me'.

JERICHA

Indeed, and giving baby up to what I would call a 'natural mother'. Alternatively ... you could try baby on solids.

JOAN

But how does this work when a newborn has no teeth?

JERICHA

You'd be surprised how many do. Cardinal had a full set.

JOAN

Well, she had double, didn't she, like a wee shark?

JERICHA

Yes, ghastly. So you'll need to put your hand into the newborn's mouth, try and get it all in, baby won't mind, and feel around, push hard against those gums with your thumb, and you'll start to meet bone, so by day three or four, baby can bite through a carrot baton and you can simply manipulate his jaw up and down.

JOAN

Like a ventriloquist's dummy?

JERICHA

Exactly.

JOAN

You do get these mothers as well, though, don't you, who chew solids like a bolognaise with a buttery garlic bread and a glass of Sauvignon, or a full roast dinner with a robust Merlot and a pud to boot, and then spit the whole lot out and into baby's mouth.

JERICHA

Yes, repulsive. I actually heard of a case where Mum was doing that with fish cakes and the child grew up thinking it was a penguin, would only wear black and white and actually went on to kill himself by dressing in a tuxedo and jumping off a cliff into the sea.

JOAN

Awful, and you have to wonder if these aren't simply bulimic mums, using their child's mouths as spittoons.

JERICHA

Very possibly so, gorging on doughnuts and Doritos and then spewing them back up. Ghastly.

JOAN

But you didn't breastfeed Cardinal, did you?

JERICHA

I couldn't, Joan, she was a very harsh biter from the get-go. Plus I've always had inverted nipples following an early fingering incident on a French campsite where my nipples retreated in shock. But your wonderful tailor Mario,* made me some magic silky pop-ins that smooth things over – or if I want to ring the changes, he's made me some pointy leather ones that will poke through a sheer top.

JOAN

Would you take the leather ones off if you were having intercourse?

JERICHA

Depends who it was with, Joan – obviously that side of things with Phillip has had to be put on hold with his Thai work, but if I was making

* See Appendix B.

love with, say, a hot Welsh lifeguard I'd keep
those on, but if the gentleman in question were
a sensitive elderly librarian, I'd probably
take them out, switch the lights off and light a
candle instead.

JOAN
And candlelight is lovely for smoothing things out?

JERICHA
Yes, although it can cast alarming
shadows Joan. I tried a candlelit approach one
night with a nervy 60-year-old virgin and,
having taken out my pop-ins, it was all going
well until he glimpsed my nipple shadows,
mistook them for two huge-beaked ducks
coming for him and fled home in tears.

JOAN
Oh dear.

'MY BABY WON'T SLEEP, AM I DOING SOMETHING WRONG?'

Yes. The main issue here is you don't want baby keeping hubby awake with its howling screams. One man compared his baby's night cries to foxes on a raping spree – and he does have a point! It's very stressful for poor old Dad, and he can't possibly maintain his high-powered job or busy golf/boozy lunch/affairs schedule if this tiny tyrant is ruling the roost with his booming night-bellows.

This is a time when Mum really needs to calm Dad down first with some energetic fellatio or by allowing him to go at her roughly front and back. Some ladies worry about burst vaginal stitches, or their abdomen re-opening after a C-section, but that's a small price to pay if hubby can get a decent night's sleep.

So now Dad's snug 'n' snoozy, let's look at how Mum can get baby off to the land of nod. Many adults have issues around insomnia or nocturnal waking and babies are no different. And just as an adult would reach for some violent masturbatory relief, drown themselves in alcohol or inject class A drugs in order to pass out, so baby needs the equivalent.

If baby is having trouble sleeping, it may well be that he doesn't like you very much. Perhaps you haven't been dressing up in a very attractive way or have failed to wear enough make-up – or you just have an irritating way about you that's causing him to stay awake at night, worrying about his future and wishing he was with another woman (just like dad!).

Too many mums are too busy thinking about number one, hoiking themselves into a tarty pleather skirt and carting their little one around so she can meet friends at a glitzy wine bar, desperate for some male attention and using the newborn as some must-have fashion accessory. Or worse, leaving it outside, whilst she gets plastered and ruptures her perineum from twerking on the tables. No one is interested in your baby and it will likely get kidnapped from the beer garden, although this may well be your secret intention. In truth mums really shouldn't venture out of the house after 3 p.m. (2 p.m. in the winter months). What you need to do is knuckle down and give baby a disciplined schedule and a regular bedtime routine.

WIND-DOWN TIMETABLE

1. Relaxing music is a nice way to get baby in the mood for a slumber. Ask him what sort of music he would like? If the answer is unclear, then you'll need to experiment. Some babies love nursery jingles (an indicator that the child won't be very bright), whilst others respond more to dirty grime (likely a future sex worker) or some bumping glam rock (tiresome travel agent).

2. Make a hot drink. Warm up a little whisky and pop it in a teat pipette. As baby goes to latch on for his final feed, pump it sharply into his mouth as a tasty relaxant.

3. You may be radiating tension in your desire to put your little one down to sleep and, again, he'll find this very irritating. So pop baby in a big warm bath and leave him to relax for twenty minutes or so with some smelly candles, whilst you do your much-needed cardio workout.

4. Make the nursery as cosy as possible. People say babies never recover from being torn from the safety of Mum's womb, so try to recreate the environment by curling him into a tight ball and place him in his cot in a pitch-black room, with no company. Remind him of Mum's heartbeat by placing a large speaker emitting a deep thumping bass drum right next to his head. Babies also miss those sloshing amniotic womb sounds, so place a small pool by his cot and sloosh the water round, or dangle him in and out, until he drops off.

5. If all else fails and baby still seems wide awake, you can always crumble up some old antidepressants which should give him a bit of a mood boost – and a couple of days of much-needed sleep.

BOBBLY BABY BONNETS: THE BOBABO

Yes, breastfeeding isn't always straightforward. For some ladies the milk isn't flowing freely from the nipple, but it is spurting happily from the vulva. This phenomenon is on the rise due to bigger, fatter vulvas as women have become increasingly greedy, snacking on fatty treats and lazing around all day. And whilst this is all rather unpleasant, it is vital that wherever the milk is coming from, baby knows he's welcome to latch on.

If you are one of these mums who are lactating from down below instead of up top, you may as well make feeding time fun with the BOBABO! These bobbly baby bonnets, covered in wobbly and textured teats, mean baby can suckle away whilst nudging his bumpy bonnet into Mum's privates, making it a great experience for both of you!

The BOBABO comes in smooth, knobbly and vibrating (if Mum wants an extra special time). And don't worry, the fast-vibrating bonnet is good for helping strengthen baby's soft new skull and acts like mini electroshock therapy, warding off any possible depression that baby might be feeling about the thought of spending his first eighteen years with you.

DO BABIES LIKE BEING SWADDLED?

Of course they do. A lot of ladies panic about swaddling, which involves crossing baby's arms right over his chest and winding him as tightly as possible in cloth, right up to the eyes – but do remember to leave the nostrils open! If you forget, simply puncture two holes in the cloth with a knitting needle, and hopefully you'll be aiming just where baby's nostrils are.

JOAN

People worry about swaddling baby too tight. But babies don't actually feel anything very much at this stage of development do they?

JERICHA

No Joan, they're completely numb until, I believe, around five or six. So even if you drop them, they simply bounce back. The number of times I dropped Cardinal – I couldn't begin to count!

JOAN

And doctors advise nowadays to swaddle baby and then hang him on a hook on the wall, as they used to do in Scandinavia?

JERICHA

Yes, you can use just a normal coat hook, Joan – or they do these pretty birth hooks in Ikea now, which can go in the hall near (or under) the coats, or simply hidden away on the back of a door. Because, let's face it, hubby doesn't want to come in and baby be the first thing he sees. He wants you, or in all honesty a prostitute, ready on all fours – and he certainly doesn't want baby taking up too much of his wall space.

JOAN

And they can sleep up there can't they? Like little bats?

JERICHA

Yes, sometimes tipped upside down, Joan, because it's actually very good for baby to get all that blood rushing to his head, particularly if he's not very bright. And then later flip him back upright like a little egg timer.

JOAN

And for hubby, you'll need baby to look nice and smell nice, so do spray his little face with perfume and some into his mouth to keep his breath fresh. And think about styling baby too.

JERICHA

Yes, maybe some nice little chinos and a Ralph Lauren office shirt for him or a leather jacket and some sockless loafers, or a body-hugging dress and pretty heels if it's a baby girl. Think about whether she's going to be an apple or a pear and so on and style accordingly.

JOAN

And for goodness sake get her on that diet if she starts getting those unsightly thigh rolls!

Keeping Hubby Happy At Your Most Unsightly

It's vital that YOU have an even hotter bod post-baby if you want to hold on to hubby and stop him straying. All these lazy ladies who think it's perfectly OK to shuffle around at home, with their ghastly mum-bob hairstyle, dangly boobs and a droopy old puss, had better think again. Once baby is two days old, it's time to get back out there, gals!

POST-BABY-BOD WORKOUT

- **The tightpuss tumblies**. This involves pushing as many marbles as possible into your vaginal vestibule and seeing if you can hold on to them as you do a series of roly-polies outside on a patch of grass, or pavement if you're not near greenery. This shows that, even though you're a dumpy new mum, you're still fun and playful. If the marbles fall out, you're obviously a bit baggy below (so try with bigger things, like boiled eggs or oranges) and if you lost the marbles altogether, it's likely they're embedded in your uterus, causing a nasty infection and possibly some toxic shock syndrome so do pop yourself down to see your GP. It's a chance to show him your vagina, and yourself as a breezy, confident mum, but please don't try and flirt if he's a handsome locum, stop kidding yourself, ladies, please!

- **The bubble-butt bouncies**. This requires you to bounce on your baggy bottom whenever you have a spare moment, to give you that sexy bubble butt that hubby will want to penetrate. For new mums who claim there's no time to spare, how about bouncing your butt up and down the stairs between cooking dinner for hubby and bathing baby? Or against the wall in that gap between some rough midnight intercourse and getting up to feed baby? Or on your seat in the local cafe in between sips of your naughty oat milk latte! Try simply bumping butts with folk in the queue at the supermarket too, as it will show that you're a lively mum and create conversation when you're likely to be at your loneliest.

- **Bangin' boob press-ups.** This means doing press-ups using just your boobs – this one's quite a challenge, and better still if you get hubby to tie your hands behind your back so you can't cheat! You'll need to use your much-weakened core to raise yourself up and down off the floor, and after a few weeks you must do this in a public place like a park or school playground, and should be able to push up using just your boobs! Try spinning round on just your nipples to show how well you're coping, maybe with some intermittent laughter.

Dealing With The Terrible Twos

JERICHA

Obviously we love to draw on our own experiences when helping some of the more hopeless mums around issues of behaviour and respect, don't we, Joan?

JOAN

Oh, indeed. Yes, my five were wonderfully well behaved and doted on me with endless kisses and pricey gifts, but Cardinal I know has been an albatross for you, frankly from the get-go. When she first went into nursery didn't she go around the room biting other children, one by one?

JERICHA

Yes, she had this enormous, and as it transpired, dislodgeable jaw. She would take a child's whole head into her mouth and try and bite it off. Eventually we sent her to this Danish man, Roben Skaarsmunde, who managed these 'running with wolves' retreats just outside Copenhagen, which allows children to burn out this feral behaviour so they return socialised and cowering, but Cardinal came back with sharpened teeth, facial bearding and frankly, ever more lupine behaviour. She started going at me in the night, hauling carcasses into the front room and marking her territory by urinating up the walls and so forth. The key here of course is that Cardinal has specific medical issues, but for the rest of you, it's likely some inherent flaw in your own personality, deep-rooted problems in your marriage, or even karmic crimes committed in your previous lives, that have turned you into an unsuccessful mother.

JOAN

'Dear Joan and Jericha, my husband and I were recently in the supermarket when our toddler Joland started throwing tins of soup around, calling me the "C-word", and kicking me in my privates. My husband didn't do anything except join in.'

From Anthea Gurpezzynoole, Dorking

JERICHA

Oh dear, well what you're actually seeing here, Joan, is Mum not coping.

JOAN

Mum's not coping …

JERICHA

And the reason poor little Joland's been reduced to kicking Mum's vulva and battering her with tins is because Dad's not getting his needs met and, quite rightly, he's joining in too. Did she say exactly how Dad contributed to the so-called assault?

JOAN

Yes, she says he was whacking her repeatedly over the head with frozen chips and then running at her, pelting her with big marrows.

JERICHA

Oh dear. Poor Gordon Gurpezzynoole's clearly not getting enough, or possibly any, sex from Mum and you can see his big frustrated balls are bulging almost out of the photo there.

JOAN

And poor wee Joland thinks he wants to batter Mum, but what he really wants is for Dad to be able to give Mum a really good going at?

JERICHA

Exactly, but my first question is why is Gordon Gurpezzynoole in the supermarket in the first place?

JOAN

I mean, could it be Mother's Day and he's joined Mum as her special treat?

JERICHA

Let's hope so. All I'd say is this is an emergency, Joan, so Mum, if this happens again, you should grab Gordon, shove him behind a display, get on your knees and gobble him to climax, because once you've done that you'll be amazed at how the temperature changes.

JOAN
And then you'll find when you get
back to little Joland he'll be happily
munching away on a carrot reciting
the alphabet.

JERICHA
Precisely, Joan.

JOAN
And then Anthea Gurpezzynoole can drive
Gordon Gurpezzynoole home
for his post-ejaculate snooze,
whilst she prepares him a big
meaty dinner.

JERICHA
And young Joland can go to his room
and amuse his young winkle with posters
of topless ladies.

We're very confident this chapter has been invaluable for nervy new mums, but if you are still unsure about your parenting skills, why not take our quiz to find out exactly what type of mother you are ...

What Type of Mother Are You?

1) You find out you're pregnant (having been trying for a long time) just as you'd booked a sky diving day for yourself and your fiancé. You're over forty so it's a high-risk pregnancy. Do you:

A) Go anyway, it was quite expensive and you can always wear two pairs of pants;
B) Offer your ticket to a friend for whom you've held long-term resentments, and hope they die on the day;
C) Have an abortion;
D) Give the ticket to your fiancé's best male friend in a ruse to see if the high-pressure environment exposes the torrid homosexual attraction you've long suspected;
E) Stay at home and have a cosy evening rubbing in your perineal butters with a bottle of Merlot and a hefty curry.

2) You're getting married days before your due date, but your religious parents just thought you were getting fat. On the wedding day, you feel your waters break!
Do you:

A) Go ahead and give birth; you can't fight nature and it's as good a time as any to let your parents in on the secret;
B) Tell everyone you've got food poisoning from the prawn cocktails and when baby comes out just say it's a big bad prawn;
C) Have an abortion;
D) Get drunk and try and have sex to cover the emerging infant – and if spotted, say it's one of the flower girls pushing for a threesome;
E) Push baby back inside and insert a little breathing straw for it. Then arrange a dinner party to break the news of the birth to your folks in nine months' time.

3) You're in hospital giving birth when you pass a small stool, which you attempt to sweep away. It lands on your mother-in-law's shoe (who insisted on attending the birth).
Do you:

A) Tell her to look down and draw her own conclusions;
B) Tell her she has brought dog poo into the hospital and that's very unhygienic, slapping her round the face for good measure;
C) Have an abortion;
D) Say the midwife did it and laugh;
E) Say baby did it.

Mostly As:
You're rather bossy and full of yourself, and the type of person people slag off behind your back. You should put the baby up for adoption before it's born.

Mostly Bs:
You mean well, but you're living a lie and will get your comeuppance probably sooner rather than later. You may even get yourself murdered on a foreign holiday.

Mostly Cs:
You know what you want, and you know when you want it – that's a great trait for new mums! Have a glass of wine and some Wotsits!

Mostly Ds:
You're very creative. Maybe think about making cards with some mentally ill people or becoming an actress.

Mostly Es:
You're going to make a great mum. Well done.

Chapter 4

WHY YOU'VE FAILED AS A MOTHER

The Spawning Of A Homosexual Child

We all dream of having the perfect son or daughter but this rarely happens. And as your little one grows, you may well continue to feel a profound sense of disappointment. Maybe your child is very boring or rather tubby, maybe the eyes are too close together or it weeps all the time, or maybe your child stinks. Sometimes it's all of the above. And sometimes your child will be gay.

It's not so trendy to be homophobic any more, but a lot of parents really don't like homosexuals and particularly Dad may want to cajole young Tommy into heterosexuality. Time and again, parents cry, 'Joan! Jericha! How did this happen?' And the truth is, in almost every case, it's Mum's fault. Often the gayness begins with lazy mothers who won't intercourse hubby, so busy are they trying to turn their sons into their own little lovers, jamming their nipples into the wee lad's mouth long past his breastfeeding days are over, only to create a deep revulsion not just towards Mum, but to women in general.

Even more dangerous are those mothers who walk about naked from the waist down, claiming to be hot because the thermostat is on the blink, filling her poor son's soon-to-be-gay nostrils with her ghastly front-botty scent and sending him, screaming, towards the nearest penis.

There are, of course, a lot of ladies who long to have a gay son and try to eat all the right foods to create one, so she can essentially birth a big doll with a willy that she can keep at home with her until she dies.

Spotting a Gay Toddler

Whilst most male toddlers will be after Lego and punching everyone (as they should be), the gay toddler will be begging for fashion items and fancy foods* and will often reach puberty much earlier than his peers. We knew of a wee chap locally, Hamish McGoggon, who had grown a full pubic triangle by the age of five, and treated guests (and the hired entertainer 'Micky Magic') to his 'big-sized-man's' ejaculation at his sixth birthday party.

Some parents try to turn a blind eye to the clearly emerging homosexual and marvel at their son's apparent popularity. What can start as Mum feeling proud he's brought a giggly gaggle of boys home for a fun playdate often ends in nasty upset when it becomes clear young Tommy was merely out to ply his grisly trade. When Mum ventures upstairs with a tray of fancy biccies and some fizzy orange squash, she will find a penis in a mouth or a penis in a bottom, or worse – lots of penises jammed into one mouth, for example, and another fleshy cluster vying to fill a solo anus.

* See page 101 for inspiration

FUN WITH FAECES

Another sign of the emerging homosexual is the little chap who doesn't want to say goodbye to his faeces, either through deliberate constipation (so he can experience the heady pleasure of the dangling half in/half out stool) or by going back to his potty to marvel again and again at the russet rainbow of his very own botty gifts. And by the time he's twelve, this guy's set up shop in the bathroom, eating all his meals and quaffing lattes beside a toilet brimming with stools.

Fully grown gay men often freeze their faeces in pretty condoms in order to engage in a practice they call 'Plop Docking'. They love to re-insert these chilly dildos either into themselves or into their partners' bottoms, to while away the hours between episodes of *Neighbours*. Often you'll see them on the heath with what appears to be a freezer bag full of yummy picnic lollies, but is in fact chock-full of big frozen stools. This practice has become so popular there are even 'Plop Dock Stops' available at motorway services nowadays for gay guys who can't go two miles without needing to engage in this practice. (And you'd be surprised how many 'straight' guys have a quick go too, whilst wifey's stuck in the fishy toilet queue, busting for a tinkle.)

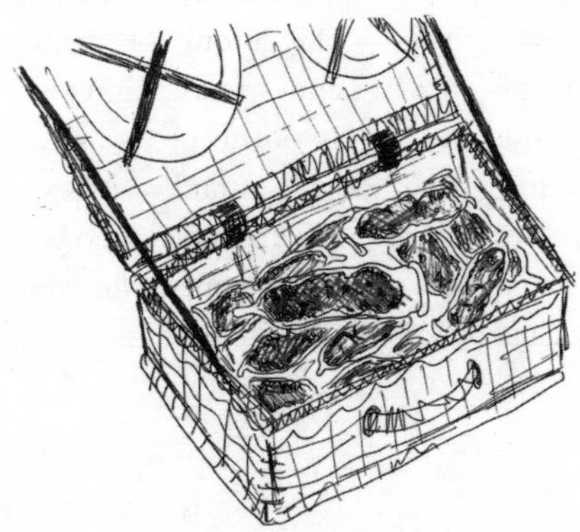

SO IS THERE A CURE?

If Mum and Dad are really intent on stamping out little Tommy's leanings, here are our top five most effective methods, as identified by *The Radio Times* magazine.

1) **Antibiotics**. Many doctors prescribe a hefty course of antibiotics, usually used to treat ghastly teen skin conditions such as acne vulgaris. But the most common school of thought, consistently confirmed through peer-to-peer trials, is that homosexuality is viral, meaning antibiotics won't have any effect and the yeasty gut caused by antibiotics can actually lead to profound acne. Meaning you then have a rather spotty and still very gay toddler.

2) **Exorcism**. Some parents will invite their priest round to exorcise what's believed to be an evil botty demon. The priest attempts to draw out said demon, enticing it from young Tommy's anus with segments of candied orange peel and other brightly coloured party foods. In more extreme cases, priests will use a snake, waved just outside the rectum, to lure the botty demon forth.

But this generally ends in tears as the snake will inevitably go straight up the anus, offering the little chap a fine old time whilst priest and parents wrestle, in a tug of war line, to pull it out. And if they succeed, the snake, full up with stools and furious at being yanked from his big brown lunch, will vomit into the faces of its assailants and then bite them to death.

3) **Straight Porn**. Some mums have looked to heterosexual starter-porn to straighten out a lopsided youngster – a sort of Ladybird book guide with lots of fun, 'lift the flap' illustrations of big porny boobs and 'scratch 'n' sniff' vulvas. But generally this will result in the young fella being ever more repulsed by ladies, and potentially turning on his own mother and trying to set fire to her genitals. Not least because some mums have resorted to shoving their own pudendas in young Tommy's face, in lieu of a kiss goodnight, hoping this might pull him in the right direction. We've even heard of some desperate housewives who offer their sons their own home 'adult' show, hefting themselves around poles whilst jiggling their ancient boobs and flicking their bean at the young buck, in a frantic attempt to swing him back towards the hetero light.

4) **Hypnosis**. 'I Can Stop You Being Gay'. Inspired by a recent visit to Paul McKenna for her recurring nocturnal bed-soiling, Cardinal attended a weekend course in hypnosis and now practices this money back if you're not 'straight in eight' (days) technique in a pop-up shop in Soho. Her programme has seen some success, especially when combined with a night crème called 'TRUMPET'. It was created by Donald Trump's father, Fred, on realising that young Donald was showing all the red-flag signs – and in fact Fred himself had been battling his own botty-urges throughout his marriage (only siring Donald after using this treatment on himself). The crème is simply applied to the anus, burning it clean away, whilst the patient listens to Cardinal's dulcet tones.

CARDINAL's 'I Can Stop You Being Gay'
As recommended by Tom Cruise.

We asked Dr Graham Nupp,* a top clinical psychologist at the Maudesley Hospital, London, England (who has done some wonderful work with Cardinal), to tell us more. As well as being a shoulder to cry on, Dr Nupp is a wonderful ballroom dancer, exquisite dresser and a sublime pastry maker. He sent us this fascinating medical report.

THE IMPORTANCE OF EARLY IDENTIFICATION OF THE HOMOSEXUAL MALE

Dr Graham Nupp, MPhil

THE GAY BABY IN THE WOMB

Studies show the homosexual baby can be spotted as early as his seventh week in-utero, and instead of the familiar knees-to-chest, curled-up 'cosy-cashew' position, the foetus will appear to be standing, hip to one side, head cocked in a bitchy manner and one hand flopping forward. Often it will be dancing.

THE HUNGRY ANUS

Through placing objects near the newborn's anus (much as you might put metal near a magnet) scientists have noted the gay baby's anus already knows it wants to ingest something, as toys and biscuits within a ten-inch radius go shooting up his bottom. This is a condition known as the 'hungry anus' (or anum esurientes), causing the rectal mouth to suck up almost anything in its path. Consequently, there have been cases of lazy mums using their child's bottom as a make-shift hoover whilst she munches her Twirl and flicks through *Grazia*.

* See Appendix B

THE RAVENOUS ANUS

For those allowed to pursue their 'natural' proclivities, the appetite can be regulated and there will be an average amount of anal activity. But in those where such hunger is suppressed, it can progress to an insatiable level of appetite that results in these hefty adult homosexual monsters, hurtling about on mobility scooters – literally disabled by a condition known as 'Ravenous Anus', or anum rapax, hurling his splayed angry bottom at everything in its path, eager to ingest it.

ANAL TRANSPLANTS

Some parents will consider having their potentially gay toddler's anus replaced. It is now possible to grow a heterosexual anus on a mouse's back, which can then be successfully transplanted. Occasionally this can backfire, as witnessed by the infamous case of the mouse whose entire face was overgrown and became simply an anus with eyes, whilst his poor twin suffered an entire patchwork of anuses in all colours and creeds, grown along his back and face. The unfortunate pair were illegally sold to a bisexual ringmaster of a touring mouse circus where they endured untold hardships, but fortunately eventually escaped and now live happily above a tailor's shop in Gloucester.

Paper published 12 May 1975.
DR G. NUPP. MB. DRCOG. DFSRH.

'MY SON IS GAY! WHAT SHOULD I FEED HIM?'

Obviously, gay guys love all the finger foods – picky, nibbly things to fondle and play with. Carrot batons dipped in chocolate, Wotsits daubed in peanut butter – anything colourful, flamboyant, mouth-sized and showy. None of your beige roasts for them, thank you very much. They like fancy, pricey nibbles to boot – geranium flowers and seaweed, with every dish more than a little dressed up! A boiled egg in a jaunty leather hat and chains. A full English with the sausage tapered and a pair of beef tomatoes nestling at the base of its shaft. And don't forget, these guys love fudge.

This following recipe is a great one if your gay guy is feeling wobbly and needs a yummy gobbly. Older homosexual men particularly love this, but little ones also tend to have quite a fussy and sophisticated palate and love showing off at birthday parties and bitching about the more conservative guests!

BOTCHED FUDGE GOBBLIES WITH CORIANDER AND GERANIUM LEAVES, SERVED WITH WINTER GOLD CRISPS AND PENIS-PATTED YUM YUMS

INGREDIENTS

You'll need:
6 pints of ram's cream
600g San Franciscan bronzed sugar
A flute of puppy butter
A slipper of lavender-smoked toffee shavings
A thimble of Egyptian gold leaf
24 Tokyo Yum Yums
Tuscan torn coriander
19 Ibizan geranium leaves

METHOD

Blend all the soft ingredients in a glitzy cocktail maker, heat in a Tom Ford toffee pan, drizzle the goo over the Yum Yums and boogie the leaves onto everything. Finally, pat generously with a big gay man's penis and plop your finished gobblies into a frosted thong.

Serve on a toned naked bottom with tequila.

'WHAT DOES A GROWN GAY MAN LOOK LIKE?'

Homosexual men are generally promiscuous and muscular, though often stumpy and bald, as the overload of testosterone has forced all their head hair down to the scrotum, creating a fat, wiry bush around tight, angry balls. Those who are not of the bald and ripped persuasion may be thin, pale and highly inquisitive. Or they may be more the pasty, plump, nervous type of gay man, who droops about the place, moaning about every little bodily twinge whilst weeping into his chai latte.

These latter types should really stay at home with Mum and try dating an elderly male relative to get into the swing of things. Alternatively, Mum can let her facial hair take hold and pose as a homosexual man, bringing her son off when necessary, just to tide him over until he's able to gain the confidence to go out to a club under some railway arches that stays open all night, and allow a real gay man to play with his anus.

WHERE DO GAY MEN HAVE SEX?

Dirty toilets are still the go-to for gay guys to nudge and poke at each other's bottoms, but frankly they are happy with a dirty anywhere, as long as there is at least a whiff of faeces in the air and the eerie yet arousing approach of the bobby on the beat. Consequently, you will often find older homosexual men paying hunky young guys in tiny shorts with oiled torsos and pierced nipples to build them small colonies of huts with accompanying long drop toilets near, or directly outside, the larger cosmopolitan police stations.

FURTHER READING

We hope this chapter thus far has helped you to care for the gay man in your life. For further reading we suggest the following books, all penned by the slight but commanding Dr Graham Nupp:

The Complete Anus
The Absent Anus
The Angry Anus
Anuses that Love Too Much
How Big Was my Anus?
He's Just Not That Into Your Anus

And for the youngsters, there's also Dr Nupp's collection of children's stories:

Little Red Riding Anus
Black Anus Rides Again
Little Anuses
Anne of Green Anus
Five Go Mad in an Anus
Pippy Long Anus
Pollyanus

WHAT DO YOU BUY THE GAY MAN WHO HAS EVERYTHING?

Obviously Mum wants to help her gay son to be the very best kind of homosexual with a nice springy anus and an ability to accommodate lots of different guys. We know what fusspots these fellas can be around birthdays and Christmas, so here's a fab stocking filler that will put a smile on any gay guy's face ...

PENI-BEANIES

PRETTY PENILE HATS FOR PROMISCUOUS GUYS who don't have time to wipe up a dribbly willy! Elasticated like a shower cap, the Peni-Beanie pops onto the end of his penis and can expand or contract with each erection or deflation as you go about your day.

The Peni-Beanie comes in:

Regular: the original best seller – in navy nylon for dads and secretly gay headmasters.

The Orlando: inspired by Orlando Bloom, this is a baggy woollen beanie, drooping off the end of the penis for the hipster homosexual, collecting all the nasties as well as hinting at a bigger penis under your trousers than you really have!

The Kemp: designed by Ross Kemp, this tight, angry beanie fits like a condom and comes in tough flipper rubber or brutal leather. Perfect for sadistic military guys, stressed businessmen and politicians having affairs.

The Noddy: a fun, floppy Peni-Beanie with tinkly bell, in harlequin silk, for advertising executives, retired men, and troubled folk who walk on motorways naked.

The Top Hat: in firm black felt, for the discerning bi-gent about town.

The Bowler Beanie: for fat-penised fellas with a great sense of humour.

The Winter Bobble: for guys with depression.

THE PENI-BEANIE can be used as part of foreplay and teased off by your partner's mouth. Make sure you nibble it off with your teeth, all the while groaning with pleasure. And do take it into your mouth, so that he doesn't have to see all that nasty gunk. Simply swallow the whole thing and carry on.

Lesbians and Where to Find One

There are fewer lesbians than there used to be due to global warming, and those that survive tend to migrate to areas with canals and fields nearby so that they can roam in herds, keeping their big vaginas damp. You'll notice even in cities such as London, the majority of them can still be found by man-made waterways, and most weekends you'll see furious lesbians pounding across the bridge at Camden in search of long, bristly vegetables. This type of canal-dwelling lesbian will have larger-than-life nipples, a ruddy face and a rather surly attitude.

THE LESBIAN IN THE WOMB

The lesbian foetus, instead of scooched up tight with her knees to her chest, will appear to be standing with her legs akimbo in a defiant 'fuck-you' stance, her little hands in imaginary dungaree pockets, often staring at the lady doing the scan in an angry but lustful manner. And almost as soon as the lesbian baby can crawl, she will be clamouring for cargo pants and key chains, her frontal hair lock suddenly springing up into a firm, randy quiff.

Just as there is the hungry anus in guys, so there is the 'Hungry Vagina' in the gay gal. In 'regular' girls the hungry vagina (esurientes vaginarum) is always looking for the penis – and has no real sense of its own existence until it finds one and ingests it. But the lesbian vagina is only greedy for its own kind.

What's little known is that the lesbian vagina has eyes. If you were to take a photo on the latest iPhone, you would see two very tiny, but nonetheless distinct, rather suspicious eyes – neither as bulbous as a frog, nor as dead as a fish, more like a spider's wary eye, one on each side of the labia, jammed next to the clitoral hood. Never closing, the lesbian vagina's eyes are always looking, waiting, plotting.

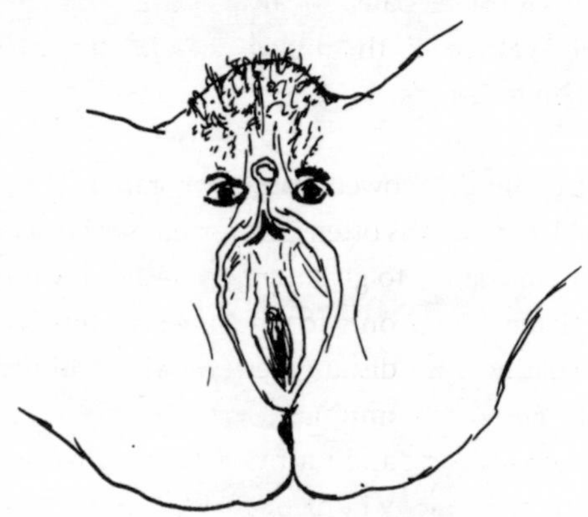

SO HOW DOES THIS CONDITION ARISE?

Once again, Mum needs to put her hand up here. The most common causes of lesbianism in tiny babies are very avoidable and there's simply no excuse for it, other than Mum's neglect. Here's what to watch out for ...

- The trigger can be something as simple as dressing baby in a blue T-shirt and combing its hair to one side. Perhaps Mum's unhappy in her marriage and is trying to create her own new little husband. Before you know it, she's drawn a moustache on baby Deborah and is trying on new bras in front of her, stripping off her dirty pants without care and generally conditioning the moustached infant to crave a life lost in big bras and crusty gussets.

- Maybe baby Deborah has been crawling around exploring Mum's bedroom, only to find her grisly collection of battered vibrators and soon develops a taste for these big chewy penises. And when she spies Dad's real life winkle, plopped like a sad slug atop his lopsided balls, she really doesn't like the look of it and greedily gathers up the dildos like a farmer at harvest, and scurries them to her cot.

- Or perhaps Mum's allowed baby Deborah to catch a nasty vaginal cold. Lazy mums often plonk their newborn lasses out in the garden sans nappy to give them some air 'down there' – but then completely forget, only to remember the tiny bundle hours later after hearing some distant mewling whilst drinking her way through the *EastEnders* omnibus. On retrieving the teary tot, the vagina will be sneezing and runny – permanently deforming its ability to enjoy the tangy honk of a penis, rendering it only ever able to truffle for pussy.

IS THERE A CURE?

Sadly, as has been proven time and again, there simply is no cure for lesbianism. It is a condition, much like male pattern baldness, that one simply has to manage. That said, there are now some (albeit pricey) lesbian care homes available for those unable to cope, where lost ladies are encouraged to loaf about all day eating peanuts and swapping key chains and Brylcreem to distract them from the muffled cries of their greedy vulvas.

How Can I Tell If I'm A Lesbian?

- Perhaps you're married to a male, yet your pelvis keeps pulling you towards the ladies in the showers at your local pool and you find yourself hungrily ogling them soaping up their big sopping bushes. Or if you're trying on some new hefty pants at M&S and the sordid sound of rustling undies in the next cubicle gets you all tingly below, then chances are Mum allowed you to suffer a nasty vaginal cold as a baby due to her inherent laziness and now you are blooming into a fully fledged *Lesbiana* lady.

- Or are you one of these dumpy, gothy girls who keeps big hamsters and, tired of assaulting household appliances, have recently foisted yourself on a drunk female chum and convinced her she's a lesbian, only to find you've ruined the friendship? And as she hasn't got the confidence to leave, you've become a lady Fritzl and locked her in your basement to do to her what you will. This type of behaviour can be a fairly clear indicator of galloping lesbianity.

- Maybe you're one of our LOLLS (Late Onset Lesbian Ladies). Sickened by your failed marriage and unsuccessful in getting off with any of your son's friends, you shock your dreary book group by dyeing your grey hair pink and parading your wizened muff around town, desperate for some portly lass to grab a munch. Again, these ladies are often to be found lurking around toilets or foisting their weathered groins on unsuspecting women at Zumba classes and high-end supermarkets.

Incidentally, if you do commit to this last path, your best bet is to go full-throttle and head to one of the large lesbian shopping outlets (usually found in the West Country or Northumberland), and get yourself kitted out in the traditional uniform. You can bulk-buy cargo trousers and keys chains, real ale kits and short-sleeved shirts for the hefty-boobed lesbian, or angry vests for the pancaked. Pants-wise, you should be looking at schoolboy Y-fronts or baggy boxers. Of course you hear rumours of these so-called 'femme' or 'lipstick' lesbians, with gamine haircuts and delicate features, who normally wear nicely tailored slacks and pretty nipple-skimming tops, with small dogs on chic leather leads, and heavily rimmed but sexy-as-hell glasses. But unless you are under twenty, an absolute corker and French, we suggest you don't try and ape their look or attempt to pursue these poor wispy girls who will only make you look like a paedophilic ogress.

WHAT DO LESBIANS EAT?

The happy lesbian enjoys bitter, claggy foods: houmous, sprouts, tuna, heavy buckwheat breads, clumpy tahini and any old vegetables left at the back of the fridge, even ones stuck to the sides. She loves to share these with other jovial gays, often with a tepid real ale and some amateur juggling. Here's a firm favourite enjoyed by Cardinal and her clan on many an impromptu canal-side picnic.

CLAGGY BUCKWHEAT AND SPROUT 'N' TUNA FLATBREAD PATTY-BOOBS

INGREDIENTS

You'll need:
A bucket of buckwheat
A large can of line-caught friendly tuna
Organic wholemeal flour
A bag of shrivelled sprouts
An elderly carrot
2 brown olives

METHOD

Fill the bath with hot water, tip in the bucket of dried buckwheat and leave to soak for a fortnight. Add the sprouts on week two. You could still technically have a bath in here if necessary, but generally lesbians don't wash.

Sift the wholemeal flour through your fingers, add a little of yours and your partner's post-sex spittle, and shape into boob-shaped patties.

Flatten your patty boobs, then toast on the grill. Some lesbians love to jig a bit to some music as they cook. It's usually just shifting their weight from one large sandaled foot to the other, but they seem to enjoy it and it's best not to disturb a big lesbian in motion.

Once lightly blackened, split open the steaming patty boobs and tip the can of tuna and soggy sprouts inside. Serve on a manly napkin with the two olives as nipples and the old carrot on the side, accompanied by a large vodka.

I'M WORRIED ABOUT MY VAGINA!

JOAN

'Dear Joan and Jericha, I'm a large lesbian in my late fifties, heavily into dogs, crafting and great red wine. I've had a couple of nice relationships but always get left, I think because of my close-together vagina and anus. Is there anything I can do?'

Jean Dumpty, Hartlepool

JERICHA

Lovely name Dumpty isn't it? Humpty Dumpty.

JOAN

Yes, and she does look like a giant egg so that's quite fun – and I imagine not a problem in the lesbian community?

JERICHA

No, they're not fussy, so your scope is widened hugely if you do decide to become one.

JOAN

And you can just decide, can't you?

JERICHA

Well, yes, you don't have to take an exam!

JOAN

So Jean's enclosed this picture here of her vagina – almost merging into the anus like a sort of letterbox really?

JERICHA

Yes. There is a hint of a very, *very* faint membrane between ... Or is that just a little piece of paper she's popped in there, Joan?

JOAN

Yes, a bit of purply brown tissue paper – that she's fashioned into a pretend perineum. But, no, I think she's got this condition called 'vaganus'.

JERICHA

Indeed, becoming rather common amongst the lesbian community and sometimes there is a link, because often these younger lesbians are very frenzied in their self-stimulation and will grab and use anything to hand, be that a candelabra or a jug.

JOAN

So, it's a bit like someone mistreating the nose with cocaine and destroying the septum?

JERICHA

Exactly, she's destroyed her botty septum, Joan, and being in her late fifties, she'll have done a lot of rubbing and bumping in her life, on the bus, on the tube, or at the seaside shuffling along the seafront walls without pants on.

JOAN

Are any lesbians actually born with a vaganus?

JERICHA

Yes, if Mum's been drinking heavily, but for some ladies it's become a fetish and they are asking to have one created surgically if they're going to have a baby – which some of these pairs of ladies do nowadays.

JOAN

But not very hygienic with all that mix of back and front.

JERICHA

No. So you will need to rinse baby under the tap when it comes out

HOW DO LESBIANS RELAX?

As we know, most lesbians are tense, angry, difficult women and Cardinal is a case in point. But it was her huge behavioural issues that eventually led her to designing the adult all-girl gym mat that has brought untold relief to many of our suffering sapphic sisters.

THE LESBIBAMA

The Lesbibama is a lesbian big baby mat designed for you to have some 'me' times. You can lie it on first thing in the morning, or at work if you're feeling stressed, or when you just want to wind down and have a lesbian play before bed.

With fun dangly corduroy dildos and big woolly vulvas, squidgy polythene boobs and swinging keys, lesbians can tug and tussle whilst the mobile plays nursery rhymes from KD Lang and soothing but sexy song stories from Joan Armatrading.

Lesbians do love to masturbate, so you may find some of the attachments go missing, but most of the Lesbibamas come with spares, as it's not advisable to challenge a lesbian about missing items.

WHERE DO LESBIANS USUALLY HAVE SEX?

JOAN

We've had a lot of questions around lesbian sex venues. We know gay men have an enduring love of sex in dirty toilets, but what about the lesbians?

JERICHA

Well Cardinal, interestingly, isn't keen on toilets in general, and has a little pot in her room that she'll defecate into and then pop outside her door.

JOAN

For you to remove?

JERICHA

Well, I have a lady that will see to that.

JOAN

Good. But is she in the minority, Cardinal, vis-à-vis lesbians and toilets?

JERICHA

I think so, Joan. I know a large herd of lesbians who do love to do things in public toilets.

JOAN

But I imagine they'd take a hygiene spray in there and maybe a scented candle to set the mood?

JERICHA

Yes, some would pop a figgy Diptyque candle on the cistern, or a cheap

Aldi copy if she's the stingy type, which many of them are – and maybe an iPod with a little speaker to create a seductive atmosphere ...

JOAN

P'raps pop a bath bomb in the toilet water for some movement?

JERICHA

Yes, that would give the feel of a sort of spa break, Joan. And then they'll have incredibly rough, violent sex.

JOAN

Well yes, I know they all carry big, often multicoloured, dildos, don't they?

JERICHA

Indeed, Joan, in their dildo-holsters.

JOAN

Wonderful. And as a feel-good, mood booster bonus, of course lots of heterosexual men love watching lesbians at work! So do keep sending those videos in, ladies.

JERICHA

But no beefy dykes, please, we've had several complaints about those, as there's only a very small pocket of demand for those from the gentleman.

JOAN

Cardinal likes those, doesn't she?

JERICHA

She does, as do fat men who do a lot of gaming and a portion of elderly chaps who've had strokes or other brain injuries.

JOAN

And of course there are sexy films for homosexual guys too, aren't there?

JERICHA

Call Me by Your Name.

JOAN

Oh yes, that was very peculiar, wasn't it? With the peach?

JERICHA

Well, you have to wonder who was going to clear all that up afterwards ...

JOAN

And with that very hot weather, I was worried sick Timothée Chalamet would get a nasty UTI after that.

JERICHA

Incidentally neither Timothée nor Mr Hammer were actual homosexuals.

JOAN

Very convincing. But thank goodness, because what a super dancer, wasn't he, Armie? Those lovely long legs.

JERICHA

Gorgeous, Joan, rangy.

JOAN
I actually saw him at an awards ceremony and he was dancing there too.

JERICHA
Was he?

JOAN
Yes, no one else was.

JERICHA
Oh.

JOAN
And he hadn't even won anything!

THE DELUDED LESBIAN

We recently had a correspondence with a large, somewhat deluded lesbian called Merry Piper. Merry waxed lyrical about what a good catch she was with her fantastic banter and enormous boobs, a common brag amongst older lesbians.*

She'd been with her partner Deborah, a big-faced woman of a similarly cubic-build to herself, for several years. Both enjoyed hiking, dogs and bread making, and were both martyrs to long, heavy periods, but Merry felt she deserved something rather prettier than the large-featured Deborah. Though not a remotely attractive woman herself by any stretch, Merry was desperate for some fun with one of these aforementioned French-looking lesbians, with the just-budding boobs, the chic little vulva, the gamine crop and the long spindly legs. And she hoped her outsize melons would seal

* A side bar here, Cardinal is also very proud of her big boobs, a common brag amongst the more smug lesbian, although hers are not strictly her own. She has had them enhanced several times by Mahmoud – his idea – in an attempt to balance things up with her outsized head.

the deal, because at the end of the day lesbians do love a big handful.

They also love an eau de parfum. So in addition to bigging up her boobs to lure her pussy prey, Merry Piper sought out a scent specifically mixed for older lesbian lasses to attract younger, fitter models and stumbled across one of Cardinal's more successful inventions, 'GUSH!'. Harvested from the genitals of promiscuous female hedgehogs, GUSH! is mixed with cinnamon, burnt carrots and deep woody whiffs with just a hint of lemon – because all lesbian ladies love a lemon. They like fish with lemon, gin and tonic with lemon and indeed revel in all things citrus, particularly an easy-peeler. Cardinal says that the way you tumble-tease the skin off the fruit is like peeling panties off a sexy rounded butt, then popping the whole juicy delight into your mouth and letting the liquid trickle down your chin.

With all this in mind, Merry ordered a big bottle of GUSH!, doused herself in it, boarded the Eurostar and took herself off to Paris, thundering about the place, lurking down alleyways in her tight beret and generally stalking these ethereal French waifs smoking their way around the city, in search of *Le Pussy*.

On several occasions Merry took herself out for a stinky meat dinner, downed several bottles of red wine and, black-lipped and bloated, hauled one of these poor spindly lasses back to her cheap hostel, in the hope of some joint vulva-fumbles, but generally ended up passing out, wasted. On one occasion, she even soiled the bed with one of her long lesbian logs,which was frankly bigger than the lass she'd brought back.

Merry wanted some of that juicy, easy-peeler action and she thought simply spraying on some GUSH! would do it. But at the end of the day, we advised her to have a bath, shave her legs, buy a decent bra and reconsider the merits of her simple life with the dowdy but dependable Deborah.

A CAUTIONARY LATE-ONSET-LESBIAN TALE

JOAN

'Dear Joan and Jericha, I've reached the menopause and have no interest in intercourse with my husband. I tried flirting with various men, such as our postman, the old disabled man who runs our chemist and a couple of schoolboys I'd berated earlier in the park, but without success – they actually threw dog mess at me. So I decided to make a move on a female friend during a coffee morning. I tried to kiss her in the toilet, but she fled with her pants still down. What am I doing wrong?'
Maria Bloorpoose, Doncaster

JERICHA

What a sorry, sorry tale, Joan. So in her case the menopause has tipped her over and turned her into a ghastly sexual predator.

JOAN

Indeed. So Maria Bloorpoose is fifty-six and the toilet friend, Patricia, that she made the move on, is seventy-three.

JERICHA

So you wonder, then, how much has this friend, 73-year-old Patricia, contributed, albeit unconsciously, to this tryst? Where was this again? Is this the park toilets near where the dog mess was thrown?

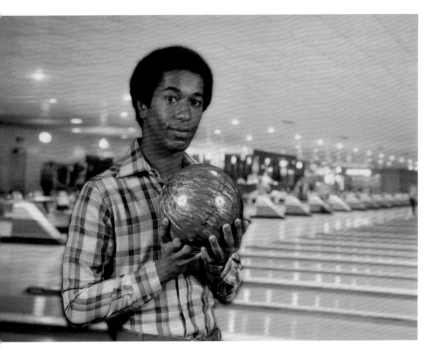

Joan's fourth husband Forrest on their honeymoon. He was rushed to hospital just after this photo was taken, as his fingers were stuck, but sadly there was nothing they could do.

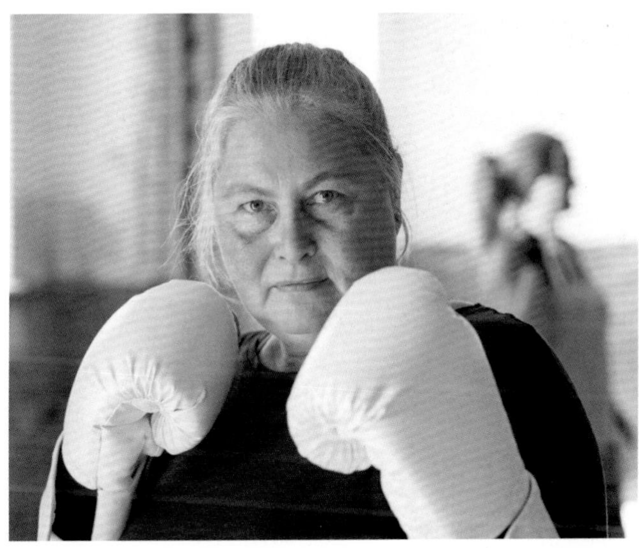

Jericha's mum Fanny Domain, in her wedding day boxing gloves.

Nose Peg Jill, sans peg, enjoying her birthday swim, as her fully made-up face and fun hat attracted a large and lively water viper into her gusset.

Jericha's synchronised swimming team cleansing their vaginas.

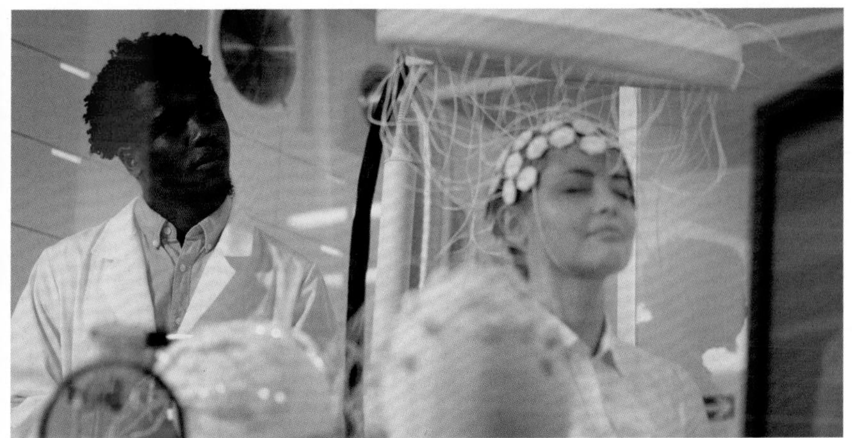

Mahmoud's fun colleague Stuart and his pretty niece Tanya demonstrating to Cardinal how a normal sized head is measured for syndromes.

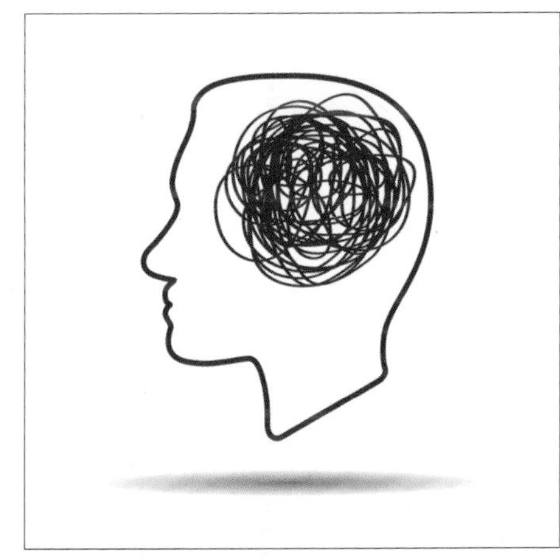

A scan of Cardinal's head reveals that it contains mostly pube-like fibres and cobwebs.

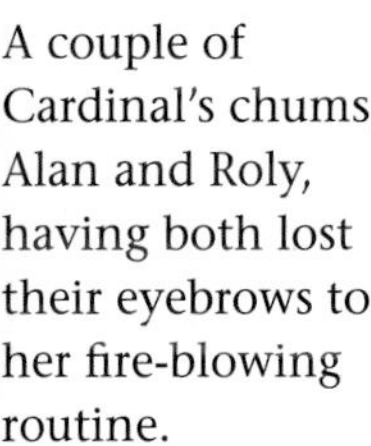

A couple of Cardinal's chums, Alan and Roly, having both lost their eyebrows to her fire-blowing routine.

Happy late onset lesbian ladies carrying their hiking dildos.

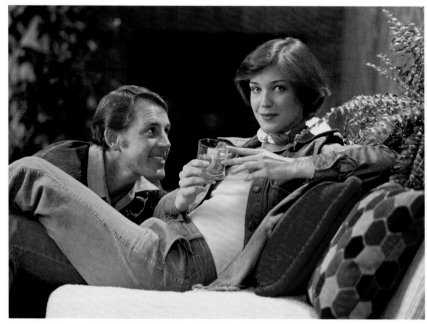

Randy Lay Vicar with engorged penis pesters his new church secretary for anal.

ßurying an ex
ınd moving
ɒn ...

Happy Christian couple pray that woman's hymen has remained intact after a strenuous ride.

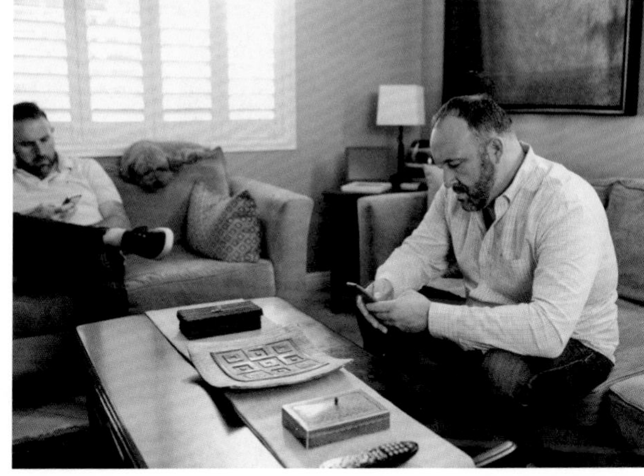

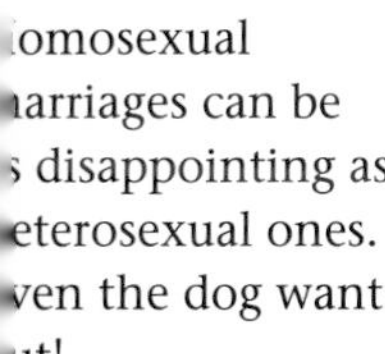

ıomosexual ıarriages can be ; disappointing as eterosexual ones. ven the dog wants ıt!

Sozzled divorcee remembers in March that she missed Christmas (again) and attempts to put things right while her son desperately signals to the photographer for help.

Selfish career lady with possessed child.

Career Mums who leave poor Dads in charge are simply storin up future problems.

Lady who ordered therapy bird but didn't check for size.

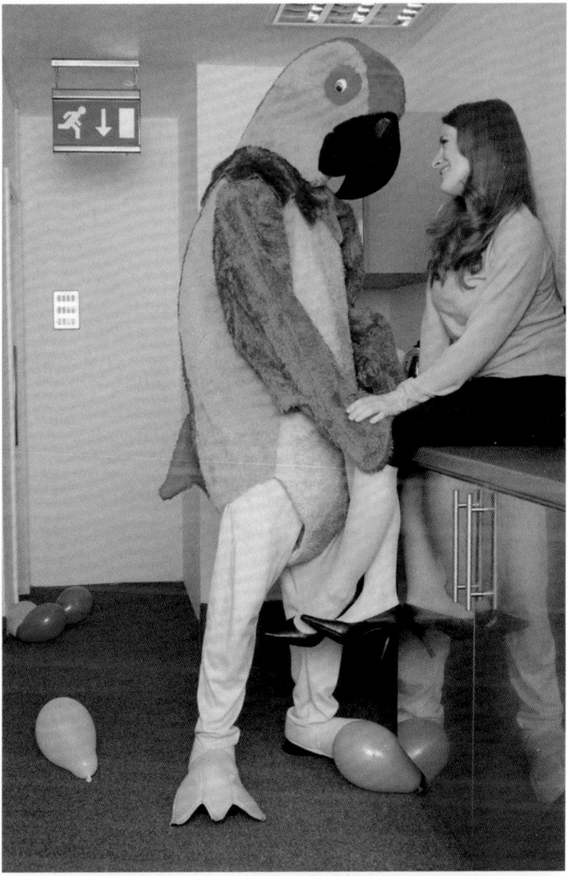

Boozy failed actress clutches Tinder date post-enforced cunnilingus.

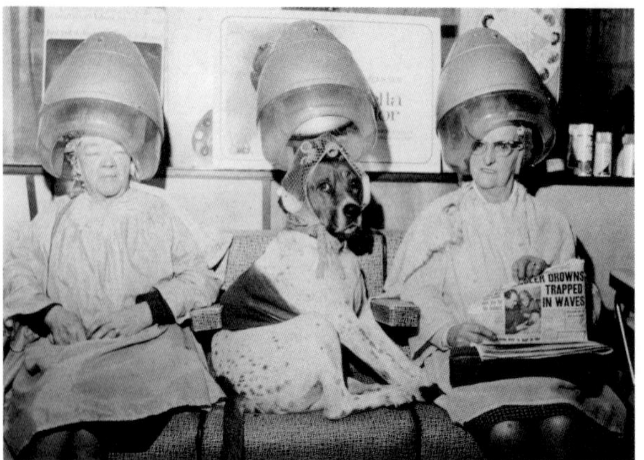

Joan's menopausal dog Sue having her weekly shampoo and set.

Koala kids – a new genetically modified breed of detachable fashion offspring available to those that can afford it!

80-year-old virgin finally finds love with a seductive young therapy dog, here talking her through the basics of CBT.

JOAN

No, it was at Maria Bloorpoose's house, in her downstairs bathroom, at the coffee morning where they were raising money for awareness around deafness. And poor Patricia is profoundly deaf herself, so I don't think she heard Maria Bloorpoose coming in.

JERICHA

You have to wonder why this Patricia lady fled with her pants still down.

JOAN

Well, in her longer letter, Maria thinks it's because Patricia was so aroused, and had created a lot of juices, despite her age, and perhaps wasn't able to pull her pants up over all the sticky discharge.

JERICHA

All the gunky mess, yes, well that's very possible Joan. We do know that as ladies age, they go through a dry phase, where the vaginal walls will crack and split, but then the body overcompensates, producing this gunky, slurpy, fluidy mess when a lady's very turned on, albeit at a deafness-awareness coffee morning. Patricia may well not have been able to manage it herself, and probably thought, Should I call for help? – hence the rushing out, pants still down.

JOAN

Yes, and probably looking for more toilet roll to mop up with, having gone through the four-pack that was sitting in the bathroom corner.

JERICHA

She's probably spotted the shower and she's thinking, Can I waddle over to that without spilling the entire gloopy contents of my vagina over the bathroom floor, slipping over and cracking my head open?

JOAN

And, of course, Maria Bloorpoose has made this move on her on the toilet, whilst this poor Patricia lady was actually trying to pass a stool. So she's stood up post-kiss, with half a stool still dangling, her panties down and covered in a snail trail ... and, for all we know, she was as keen as Maria was.

JERICHA

Yes, I'm wondering if this half-stool lady ran away mostly because she was overcome with desire?

JOAN

Well, Maria kindly sent in a video of Patricia running down the driveway with her pants still round her knees and that half-stool wagging.

JERICHA

Dropping little brown chunks as she runs, with this snail trail following her and causing a sticky, death-trap ice rink for all the other confused deaf ladies fleeing the scene behind her.

JOAN

They're all slipping over in it as they try to exit the deaf-awareness coffee morning, shouting at each other to warn them, but of course nobody can hear!

JERICHA

I think this is an instance where, all right, Maria Bloorpoose could give Patricia a call ...

JOAN

Though she is deaf ...

JERICHA

Well, she'll have one of those special loops, Joan, and potentially they could enact part two of their erotic lesbianic journey.

JOAN

With or without stools. Or Maria could look to her own marriage and say, 'OK, turns out I'm not off sex, I'll force my dry vagina on hubby's old stalk and see if I can't get myself off thinking about half-stool Pat.'

JERICHA

And show hubby the footage, it may well be right up his alley too.

We feel very confident that this chapter, guided in part by the nimble-toed Dr Nupp, has been of huge assistance to anyone whose lives have been affected in any way by homosexuality – and to whom we offer up our profoundest sympathies.

We do receive hundreds of letters asking about bisexuals, pansexuals and all the rest, but as far as we know these people don't really exist, so have decided not to include them.

Chapter 5

WHY HE NEEDS TO SLEEP WITH PROSTITUTES

Keeping The Marriage Alive

A lot of lazy ladies seem to think once they've got a ring on it and pumped out a couple of sprogs, they can sit around in elasticated trousers and stained Uggs, piling their way through packets of Yum Yums and flicking their beans to *Magnum P.I.* re-runs all day. Yes OK, you got the guy and bagged the whopping house, but don't forget, whilst hubby is beavering away bringing home the bacon, he is also being offered constant opportunities to stray with horny hotties from all around the globe. Because what lady on a conference wouldn't like to be pumped at, doggy style, by a rotund and hairless businessman? Your job now is to make sure he is properly catered for, 24/7, in order to help him say 'no' to these endless propositions.

Your Work Has Only Just Begun ...

Here is our simple three step guide for hubby's perfect morning.

5 A.M. WAKEY-WAKEY WILLY WARM-UP

JOAN

So, you wake up, blurry eyed, your
nighty's ridden up around your body—

JERICHA

And that will need to be a very
slutty nighty by the way, Joan ... so yes, your

morning bottom's exposed, and hubby's going to wake up and see that and assuming you've kept it trim, he's going to be starting to want to fidget around that quite swiftly.

JOAN

And so you need to get into gear immediately?

JERICHA

Pretty swiftly, Joan, because if he doesn't get what he needs first thing, he's going to stray.

JOAN

That day or ... ?

JERICHA

He'll stray by lunchtime.

JOAN

Gosh, OK, so he's fidgeting around with your botty ...

JERICHA

Yes, and he'll be going at that anus, Joan, which is nice and tight because it shrivels during the night, as we know. So he'll probably want to poke his penis in there first ...

JOAN

Now I know a lot of ladies worry about this sort of activity, with their morning faeces all queuing up in there.

JERICHA

Yes, the overnight, bunged-up, budged -up back passage. But look, the good news is the sphincter is semi-paralysed first thing.

JOAN

OK ...

JERICHA

So once that penis starts going in and out, yes, there'll be a bit of loosening, possibly a tiny bit of a stool perched on the end of his penis there, but you can distract him.

JOAN

Maybe pop a boob in his mouth?

JERICHA

Yes, pop in a boob, whilst deftly swapping his penis from your anus and up into your vagina where he can deposit that little stray stool without ever knowing.

JOAN

Or you could take his penis into your mouth if he's pushing for fellatio?

JERICHA

Yes, he may well want to wave his willy in your face anyway, so do just nibble that off and he's none the wiser.

JOAN

What about stool-breath?

JERICHA

You can sneak in a bit of breath spray, which you'll obviously have by your bed.

JOAN

Well anyone with a proper sex life will have all their sprays lined up on the bedside table, won't they?

JERICHA

Indeed. You'll have your vaginal spray, your anal spray, your mouth spray, your ear spray because increasingly men are going at the ears, Joan ...

JOAN

And the nose has become very popular to intercourse.

JERICHA

Yes, so bigger-nostrilled ladies are having a bit of a comeback.

JOAN

Fab. So, back to hubby's morning routine!

JERICHA

OK – and incidentally you should have set the alarm for that, it's not his responsibility.

JOAN

But most men will have wanted something in the middle of the night as well?

JERICHA

Yes, a sleepy time penile massage, maybe a little 69 midnight treat. Again the emphasis is on you; he doesn't want to have to bother with any licky business when he's half asleep, but certainly his member will need a bit of cajoling and encouragement during the night in order that he wake up feeling manly.

JOAN
And able to face the day, otherwise
he won't be able to do his job, he
won't earn any money and everything
will collapse.

JERICHA
Could even lead to his suicide, Joan,
which you really don't want on your plate.

STEP TWO: 6 A.M. WHIP HIM UP A FATTY BREAKFAST

Well done! Hubby's had his vigorous morning session, and now it's time for you to make him a big yummy breakfast whilst he 'drops the kids off at the pool'. So how about taking inspiration from Joan and her loyal driver Brian,* by whipping hubby up a belly-bulging breakfast to set him up for the day ...

BRIAN'S FATTY BREAKFAST

I'm very fond of Brian, my driver, as he's seen me through so much over the years. He's my big tubby teddy bear that's witnessed the tears behind the glamour, the grimace behind the smile, the stench beneath the perfume. But that stench unfortunately is mostly Brian, as he breaks wind almost continuously and there are times where I've felt I've had enough. I can't think of any other celebrity who would endure being driven to work in a toilet. But I know Brian can't help it and has had to have a steering wheel fitted in the centre of the dashboard as he's s'big

* See appendix B.

now, each dimpled buttock filling a seat and a chubby hip chafing at each door.

Poor Brian's had most of his colon removed and they found within it pounds and pounds of compacted stools, comprising mainly of fried bread, old sausages and pubic hair. But he doesn't regret those greasy beige brekkies with a sweet milky tea and a packet of Rothmans, nor the hours he would spend straining in a Portaloo to eject grey old pellets of long bacon rind and blood. And in honesty, we'd all eat these fatty feasts every day if we could. It's definitely what hubby needs after his morning 'workout'!

You'll need all the traditional ingredients you'd expect in a full English, but simply envelop it all in a giant pastry slipper and deep fry. Sprinkle with a Flake, a big blob of cream and you're away. Serve with sweet milky tea. Cigarette optional.

Now hubby's had some morning relief, a big fatty feed-up and passed his first bowel batch, he won't be grouchy from any poopy back-up poisoning his system!

STEP THREE: 7 A.M. POST-BREAKFAST ORAL

Fellatio, BJ, smoking the pink cigar, playing the skin flute or the two-headed woodpecker: this is number one on any guy's list, and when first dating, so many ladies trick their fella into thinking she loves nothing more than to gulp his willy down her gullet and guzzle on pints of sperm 24/7. But the second the confetti has fallen, she deems it perfectly acceptable to step that right down to a half-hearted gobble on special birthdays and every other Christmas. Some ladies never do it again, EVER. And then they wonder why their marriage fails!

JERICHA

You'd be surprised, Joan, at the number of lazy ladies out there who either won't do this, or aren't doing it properly ... who, for example, aren't taking the entire penis and testes into their mouths.

JOAN

Because they don't want to?

JERICHA

They'll say their mouth isn't big enough ... Other ladies claim that their neck got tired after a few bobs up and down. It's absolute nonsense.

JOAN

And very selfish. So, how many willy bobs and sucks should a lady be doing?

JERICHA

I think the recommended average per session is 12,000, Joan.

JOAN

OK, so 12,000, but more if he hasn't ejaculated?

JERICHA

Oh yes, you must always carry on to the bitter end, Joan.

JOAN

We've had some ladies complaining about their husband farting in their face when they're doing this?

JERICHA

Yes, this is perfectly natural and very healthy, because the lady's fast bobbing action will get everything shifting again, so he'll be gearing up to pass his second morning stool by blasting some hot wind over the waiting faeces.

JOAN

Super. But for ladies with actual neck injuries we do have the 'Blowie Brace', don't we?

JERICHA

Yes, ladies with arthritis or neck cancer are welcome to use this device. It's adapted from the traditional medical whiplash neck-brace and has a small motor hidden in the pretty fabric – and that will simply nod your neck up and down, slowly at first, then increasing in speed, until the gentleman climaxes.

JOAN

But do be sure to switch it off!

JERICHA

Yes, that will be very off-putting if he's had his milky climax and he's trying to sleep, only to find this ghastly sperm-faced lady still juddering away next to him.

JOAN

So that's the 'Blowie Brace' but there's also the 'Noddy Gobbler'?

JERICHA

Same principle, Joan, though the Noddy Gobbler is a little more pricey and that comes in more fun, gaudy colours for younger women or actresses – these show-offy types, wanting to make a statement.

JOAN

These sound fab, and great gifts for mums and aunties. Now, ladies often ask, aside from gulping as much of the willy down as they can, should they be doing anything complicated with their tongues?

JERICHA

Yes, she'll need to incorporate at least two maypole swirls up and down the shaft, two rounds of house-painter (the traditional up-and-down lick), two rounds of the alphabet and two rounds of flicky lizard.

JOAN

And should she attempt the 'frog 'n' fly'?

JERICHA

The frog 'n' fly is very nice for the more advanced, Joan, and will certainly keep your man interested.

JOAN

So that's as if you're catching flies in between flicks?

JERICHA

Yes, and do let your fella see that, keep his eyes nice and busy.

JOAN

So that's a quick helmet bob 'n' gobble, then look up at him coquettishly as you flick your tongue into the air as if you're trying to catch a fly, then back to your bobbing?

JERICHA

You've got it, Joan. Incidentally try not to catch any actual flies as he won't want those on his penis.

JOAN

No. Although Ralph used to love spiders up and down his willy.

JERICHA

Yes, I remember that.

JOAN

It started by accident one night when he found a daddy long legs sitting on his helmet and he loved it so much I'd have to catch as many of those as I could, but then he wanted little spiders as well and it got to the point where I was sneaking round people's attics! Now the other FAQ is: should I be swallowing semen?

JERICHA

This makes my blood boil, Joan! Of course you should swallow his semen! I mean, these ladies who think they can subtly turn away and spit it on to the bed or onto the floor!

JOAN

It's just rude.

JERICHA

It's very rude and it's not good housekeeping, Joan, he doesn't want a big glompy patch of spittle and sperm on the sheets.

JOAN

Now obviously some guys eject up to a pint of sperm a time?

JERICHA

Sometimes two.

JOAN

And ladies say, 'Oh, I just can't get it down.'

JERICHA

Nonsense, they should be practising with another substance of similar consistency in their spare time.

JOAN

So a clumpy custard?

JERICHA

Yes, or some old gravy. Just go off into the kitchen, get your jug and keep practising until you can get that straight down your gullet without gagging.

DAYTIME TOTTY BOOSTERS

So now hubby is suited and booted and ready to do his important job in the City. He's had his three-step morning and perhaps even a bonus eyeful of the sexy au pair, skimping about in her tiny bumbum shorts and saucy crop top, with a cheeky flash of underboob, prompting hubby to give her a sneaky botty-slap and mini vulva stroke as she bends down to wipe the skirting boards. All of which will put an extra manly spring into hubby's step and another nice lump in his pants.

Now it's time he went to work! But, ladies, your job doesn't end there ...

JOAN
When would our lady next need to furnish hubby with some sexual activity? Could she have a coffee break?

JERICHA
No. I would say she could have a quick kale juice or a small sprout smoothie, but throughout the morning you want to be sending him images of your vulva, and ideally the anus too.

JOAN
OK, so you'd use a selfie or belfie rod to take those pics?

JERICHA
Yes or the bumfie rod.

JOAN
OK, and where can you get your bumfie rod?

JERICHA
Boots do a wonderful bumfie stick, Joan, or you can go online and get same-day delivery.

JOAN

Wonderful.

JERICHA

Yes, so throughout the morning send him your sexy bumfies.

JOAN

Some ladies worry, if they've been together a couple of years, will hubby still want to look at my vulva? How do I make it more interesting?

JERICHA

Look, men love a vulva.

JOAN

But they also like variety.

JERICHA

They do, Joan, so look, we all do these Macmillan bake-off coffee mornings, and this is where you can ask friends to exchange vulva shots.

JOAN

And pretend it's yours?

JERICHA

Either pretend it's yours, or it's quite a thrill for a husband to see a variety of different vulvas from a cancer coffee morning when he's in a stressful work meeting.

JOAN

You could have a little booth for everyone to pop in, make it fun?

JERICHA

Exactly, the 'Bumfie Booth' or the 'Front Botty Booth'.

JOAN

And would you then meet him at lunchtime for a quickie?

JERICHA

Yes, hubby needs his lunchtime treats, ladies!

JOAN

Now some ladies complain of having to look after children or a dying relative or what have you, and say they can't fit this in.

JERICHA

More fool them – but if that's the case you will need to book him a prostitute to get his needs serviced and there's some gorgeous ladies out there.

JOAN

And keeping hubby sexually pumped throughout the day means he's going to be a much happier bunny when he comes home.

JERICHA

Precisely, but do be sure to be ready on your knees, heavily made up, with your mouth wide open the moment he walks through that front door, so he can let off some steam after his difficult day of pastry-filled meetings and big boozy lunches.

Why It's So Much Harder For Guys

The fact is, with all the accusations flying around nowadays, these poor guys need these sexual snacks like little good-boy choccy-drops more than ever. Prince Andrew being a case in point, poor lamb – still devastatingly handsome with his ghostly grey hair and haunted face but stripped of his dignity, and people saying he's not very bright. He's actually a lot bloody brighter than people say he is. He asked if he could have a go at our quick crossword at a charity event, and he did it in just under four hours, with very few tears. But how can these poor guys show a lady he's even interested these days if he can't have a quick grab and poke?

We've seen a huge decline in the number of men pinching at our vulvas or nudging at our boobs and it feels like we're living in an oppressive regime. Nobody's allowed to finger anybody without writing a letter first.

THE GROINAL BRAIN

We've all heard about the Gut Brain that guides us emotionally, but what is largely ignored is the Groinal Brain, which is tucked just behind the penis, and in days of yore would have been the size of a nice hefty cabbage. Nowadays, very sadly, it has shrunk to around the size of a withered old sprout, due to the fact that these poor guys have been forced to largely suppress all natural impulses, thanks to this whole ghastly 'Me Too' movement.

This is, of course, tragic, because essentially this Groinal Brain is like a tiny troll giving the guy very basic messages about what his penis needs to do that day, where it wants to go, and what it wants to go into. Such as:

PENIS AT THE CINEMA

Yes, of course the penis wants to go into a vagina or an anus, but sometimes it may just want to go shopping, have a mooch around an art gallery, or simply have a rest at the cinema. It's not always about it pumping and grinding. But because of these bitter, make-up-free feminists and angry, out of work actresses, it's lost its way and is causing not just groinal brain shrinkage but actual penile shrinkage.

NO JUNK IN THE TRUNK?

Ladies nowadays tend to be very indiscreet, discussing their husband's shortcomings (or long-comings!) with all and sundry. Maybe Busty Belinda across the way has a hubby who's very blessed below and what starts as giggly girlie fun guzzling crates of Prosecco and exchanging fun willy stories, becomes you lying awake later, wishing your fella had more junk in his trunk. Ladies, please! Of course we all love big willies, but frankly, you should be happy with any member.

TALES FROM OUR DOWN-UNDERS

JOAN: With all my husbands and the myriad wonderful lovers I've taken over the years, I've had the joy (and sorrow) of seeing an enormous range of men's downstairs danglies. I've certainly bumped uglies with the best of them and goodness what a range there is! I've talked before about the profound disappointment I felt on my first rummage in Ralph's boxers, it took me a good half an hour to locate anything, and on finding it, it was very small and very purple (which I later discovered was an underlying heart issue). But I took a deep breath, got to work and set about bringing the beast to tears, only to find it produced this rather gruesome yellow semen, which tasted just awful. But he was my man and I learnt to work with it. And as Jericha has explained, it's all part of a bigger health condition, which soon came home to roost with his cluster heart attacks and consequent 'turtle coma' – so called because he goes in and out of it. I'm just so glad I don't have to do any of that business any more, God rest his soul (he's not dead yet, bless him, but as good as). So unlike you, I now have legitimate reason to look elsewhere, to go window-shopping as it were, and yes, sometimes I may need to make a purchase or two.

JERICHA: It's no secret that I have an extremely long vaginal vestibule, leading almost to my sternum, meaning I really need a guy with a lot of length at 22 inches or more. Phillip's penis sadly isn't 22 inches and anyway, with his almost constant absence, I've had to find other ways to keep my lengthy canal in good working order. Fortunately Mahmoud, with his huge glossy fingers and long, long nails can offer me his bespoke weekly smear service – and he even supplied me with huge, jumbo-flow, silk tampons which he handcrafted for me during my menstrual years. I would often have to call on him to remove those with his special tongs, as there was so much to haul out. But it meant plenty of opportunities to spend time together, particularly on my heavy-flow days! Nowadays I am forced to keep Mahmoud's recommended 'little black book of lengthy lads' close at hand, to avoid the otherwise inevitable onset of vaginal sealing.

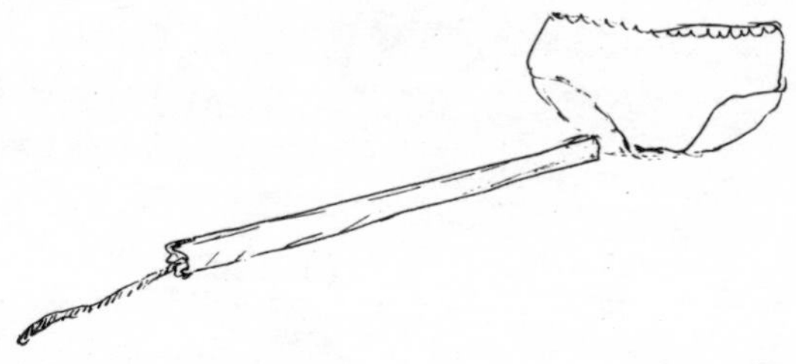

THE UNDERFED PENIS

It's all very trendy now for ladies to criticise men's genitals, but you need to ask yourself how *you* may be contributing to his lack of length! Studies show that if you compare a vegetarian man's penis to a carnivore, you'll find it's floppy and snowy white, with a droopy, weepy end – and to hold it feels like snatching at a cold, used condom.

Conversely, the carnivore's penis will be hot, fat 'n' chunky and bright, bright red, like a fire engine. So you'll want to be feeding your guy with lots of dirty, stinky stews and big, fatty puds to keep his member fit 'n' fun. By filling his tum you'll be chubbying his downstairs department and sending him into a torpor, so he won't have the energy to stray! And when he does come round, you can hop aboard his hot red dicky and ride him til supper time!

THE MOCKED PENIS

Just as the penis can shrink in cold water, so it can also shrivel away if continually exposed to unpleasant looks or the mere presence of a naggy old shrew, who's simply got too big for her boots.

RHINOPHALLOPLASTY

JOAN
'Dear Joan and Jericha, my husband
wants to get a penis extension, is
this possible? I hope so!'
And that's from Harriet Prunnybus
in Wittering.

JERICHA
Morning, Harriet – lovely beach in
Wittering. Big queues for the car
park though, so it's worth setting off early …
Now I notice she doesn't
say what her budget is?

JOAN
So you're assuming she'll pay?

JERICHA
Well, look, she's going to benefit
directly from this op. Joan, so it seems
fair. Is there a photo?

JOAN
Yes, Neil Prunnybus has kindly
draped his penis along a piece of
paper for us and popped a ruler nearby.

JERICHA

Yes, or Harriet has. I see … mmm …

JOAN

Oh dear … I certainly wouldn't want that to go anywhere near me.

JERICHA

No, you wouldn't want it … in you … particularly. But you do have to wonder, does Neil want the extension or is this all about Harriet Prunnybus?

JOAN

Yes, she could well have sedated poor Neil and scraped his flaccid winky onto that paper, which is actually quite abusive.

JERICHA

It's nasty, Joan. But look, in case there are genuine single guys out there needing this help, let's look at the three options available for the little-willied. There's the pump, the injections or the rhinophalloplasty.

JOAN

I thought that was a nose job?

JERICHA

Well, actually, the penis is a type of nose.

JOAN

Right, OK, a sort of trouser nose?

JERICHA

Yes, it actually smells.

JOAN

Oh, they always stink.

JERICHA

I mean the penis itself has the ability to smell, which is why it seeks out the heady whiff of a young flowery fertile vagina.

JOAN

Rather than these beefy old stinkers?

JERICHA

Exactly. So this is a fifteen-minute op, where a type of putty is stuffed inside the skin of the penis, much like stuffing a sausage.

JOAN

And where does one get this putty?

JERICHA

It's from snail fat, Joan, so if you think about when the snail pops his head out of his shell and does that sort of slow rearing, this mimics the engorging penis in that sense.

JOAN

OK. And so Harriet Prunnybus wants her husband's penis to rear?

JERICHA

Well, I should think she'll be after a rearing and a widening, Joan.

JOAN

Now the pumps are obviously cheaper than the op?

JERICHA

Yes, so he could try the manual type like the old balloon pump, but that will often fly off and doesn't get much purchase. Or the foot pump is better, but very heavy and will clank about in Neil Prunnybus's manbag all evening, which rather gives the game away.

JOAN

But should they use it, will Neil Prunnybus's penis expand?

JERICHA

Yes, but only for twenty minutes, then it shrivels quickly like a burst balloon leaving him with very baggy skin.

JOAN

Harriet Prunnybus says they've also tried a type of therapy where you get very angry with the penis ...

JERICHA

Yes, Ralph tried that, didn't he?

JOAN

He did, with the guy who owned our local curry house, and we'd go to his house and he'd shout at Ralph's penis for an hour every week, £400 a session, and on the final session he bashed at it with a toffee hammer.

JERICHA

And that made it bigger?

JOAN

No, it actually knocked bits off,
but we got free bhunas for a month.

JERICHA

Well, Neil Prunnybus's only other option is the womb secretions from a flat fish, like a John Dory, and then Harriet can rub that fishy discharge all over Neil's tiny penis.

JOAN

And what will that do?

JERICHA

It creates a very angry, allergic reaction and the penis puffs up in a fury.

JOAN

Fantastic!

JERICHA

And stays that way for up to three hours and then becomes very sore with all these bumpy, weepy pustules.

JOAN

But Harriet Prunnybus will have got a good three hours out of that angry one-eyed tomato.

JERICHA

Indeed. Lucky lady.

We learnt that shortly after this Neil's penis unfortunately exploded.

Why Has My Husband Gone Off Me?

A lot of guys can start to feel seriously duped as the woman they wed not only isn't keeping up to speed with her semen drinking, but seems to be collapsing before their very eyes – failing to regain her figure post-baby, either through gorging, downright laziness, or an unwillingness to save up for appropriate surgery. This is very distressing for hubby who, quite rightly, feels utterly betrayed. But what else turns him off? Sometimes it's what seem like the little things ...

PERIOD PANTS!

Many women have pairs and pairs of what they call their 'period pants'. Big, unsightly pants that they wear around their monthly 'curse' time, thinking nothing of rinsing these out and hanging them on the front room radiator, month upon month, exposing this poor guy's eyes to the myriad, sad, Branston-brown and autumnal streaks of your ghastly gussets whilst he tries to eat his TV dinner.

These large, unsightly pants then become something of a comfort blanket to the lazy lass and suddenly her underwear drawer is bulging with big, stained, baggy pants for everyday wear! Gone are the semen-splattered basques and sex-torn suspenders, goodbye slutty miniskirts and hooker-heels, here come the hospital pants, orthopaedic pumps and shapeless trews in mushroom hues!

The sad fact is, wives are simply not taking care of themselves for their men. And far too many ladies don't seem to understand how 'The Supers' like Cindy Crawford, Claudia Schiffer or Naomi Campbell look exactly the same now as they did at twenty, despite them now all being in their early seventies. Well, tell you what, these women make the effort – through seven-hour daily workouts, life-threatening cosmetic procedures and regular bingeing and purging – to maintain the gorgeous looks of a pubescent schoolgirl.

'I've tried, but it's so hard to find the time!' we hear you grizzle, as you parade your dumpy physique, proud as punch, shuffling about the kitchen with a big, cottage-cheesed bottom and aprons of jellied tummy skin spilling over your giant stained pants, whilst making poor hubby his tepid morning coffee.

Many of you smug-marrieds have sunk pretty low into a general sloppiness around grooming, with some bizarre presumption that your fella actually enjoys seeing the wizened hairs sprouting from your chunky calves and jostling out the sides of your pants, which have descended so cruelly from the filthy, fuck-my-butt thongs and peephole bras that snared your hunky groom, to underwear frankly more suited to a lady in a hospice.

MEN AT WORK

You can well imagine with this depressing, frigid, brown-gussetted harridan lurking at home, hubby will be getting very irritable and disillusioned. Ladies ask us, 'So should I start trying to introduce date nights? Some special "just us" time to try and keep him keen?' The answer is a very firm 'NO!' The last thing poor hubby wants is to have to get washed after a busy day at work, where he may well have developed 'brie penis' from his lunchtime fiddlings, and will certainly have a very whiffy 'conference anus' from smudging his sweaty unwiped botty about on the seat through all those tedious meetings. Ladies, please! He's exhausted, so don't force the poor fella to have to get changed into 'something nice' to wear to a restaurant for a wordless meal (or worse, the theatre!).

THE **BOOB HUNT** HOLIDAY

Invented by Bear Grylls and overseen by Sir David Attenborough, the **Boob Hunt** Holiday is a real lads-travaganza. A big boozy coach ride to Dover sees these middle-aged fellas throwing up en route as they shout and leer at any boobs they see on the coach or through the coach windows, splaying their greasy buttocks against the glass in response!

Once in the cafe area at motorway services, there are bonus points and extra drinks for those fearless fellas that take a good grab at a boob, or even try and go in for a cheeky suckle on a lady's nipple as she queues for her coffee.

Then it's all aboard the ferry and out at sea, the **Boob Hunt** really begins as these men, often in their mid-fifties and beyond, lurch around the ship, thrusting their tubby groins at as many boobs as possible. Many a lady pensioner will find herself wrestled to the ferry floor and mounted by these leery lickers on the loose. And guys can win a crate of ale or a hamper of stinky cheeses if they manage to ejaculate on, or near, a boob somewhere between Dover and Calais.

Once in France, they need to get as many photos of themselves with boobs in their mouths or up their bottoms as possible and if you're willing to pay that bit extra, Bear Grylls will join you for your final evening out on the town, often keen to initiate some of the more dubious activities.

The weekend is rounded off with a slightly merry Sir David Attenborough judging the **Boob Hunt** footage and presenting the winner with the **Big Milky Boob Award**, a wonderfully rounded, nipple-tipped trophy, which all the guys will love to masturbate over once Sir David has gone to bed.

Long gone are the days when he can look forward to you trussed up in a whorish dress, with towering heels and a glistening naked undercarriage. Now you have the cheek to waddle downstairs in your frumpy beige sack with a wide clumpy shoe and some unwashed Spanx and expect him to announce 'you look nice'. Once in the restaurant, many a lady uses the ghastly silence, punctuated only by hubby's weary farts, as the time to pull out her ten-year list of resentments to work through, turning 'date night' into the evening from hell. No, that particular ship, ladies, has very much sailed. And you don't even have the common decency to fellate him once you get home!

So what's the answer? Well, sometimes it's about putting yourself and all your petty grudges aside and thinking what would really make hubby happy? Well, guys like boobs, guys like beer, guys like holidays (with guys) so why not send him off on an all-expenses paid Boob Hunt Holiday!

If hubby comes back from this holiday and he's still a bit of a Forrest Grump on seeing the suicidal sight of your grim hangdog face and further dowdied frame – and if you're unwilling to go under the knife to save your marriage with some giant bowling-ball 'bolt-ons' and a full vulval transplant – then you'll need to look into regularly paying for hubby's sex workers or encouraging him to have a dirty fling with Karen, the new office intern who you know he's already been bombarding with dick pics.

For some guys though, even these 'alt sex' options are a tad too demanding and he simply doesn't have the time or energy. In which case, a wonderful gift from you and a way to ease his understandable frustrations is simply ...

The Riding Puss

JERICHA

These poor guys just need to put their penis somewhere, Joan. For goodness sake! They battle these constant urges.

JOAN

Of course! They used to say having a penis is like being chained to a lunatic!
So, this 'Riding Puss' is just wonderful. It's a 'go anywhere' device – with an orifice?

JERICHA

Indeed, so the guy can just attach it to his laptop, squirt in some gel and it has the realistic sticky flaps and gullies in there of a lady's vaginal vestibule, which will warm and pulse as hubby pumps in and out and in and out and in and out—

JOAN

Gorgeous. And he would do that in the gents at work?

JERICHA

Or if he's got his own office he can simply do it there, Joan.

JOAN

So ladies wanting to buy these for hubby as a birthday prezzie or as a stocking filler are asking: are they hairy or shaved?

JERICHA

Well, we did some market research, Joan, and it's probably not a surprise to find that most men find pubic hair physically repulsive.

JOAN

Yes, so these are predominantly bald?

JERICHA

Except for the 'Bushy Puss' for guys with a fetish. But these are usually fat guys who do a lot of gaming and still live at home with Mum.

JOAN

And there's also the kind you can just have hidden inside your trousers?

JERICHA

Yes, the 'Trouser Puss', and we also sell the 'Puss Trousers' to go with it.

JOAN

Fab. So how does this work?

JERICHA

Well, you'll be wearing your Puss Trousers, Joan, and you simply reach down, pop the Trouser Puss up and over your penis as you sit at your desk, and you can then have a full intercourse experience whilst you're working.

JOAN

So OK for the boss, but not great if you're in an open-plan office?!

JERICHA

Well, this is the beauty of it, actually, Joan. It has a spring mechanism so it moves itself.

JOAN

So, like having a lady on top riding you?

JERICHA

Exactly, it's like being ridden at your desk, Joan, hence the name Riding Puss, so a man can happily pump away until he climaxes and hold an important meeting at the same time. And even in an open-plan office he can move around with it quite happily popped in his Puss Trousers. So he's free to stroll to the water cooler, or stand at his raised desk walking machine and no one need ever know he's enjoying a nice round of intercourse!

JOAN

But watch out for your 'sex face', guys!

JERICHA

Yes! Though you can explain it away afterwards saying you had some trapped wind.

JOAN

Or were very excited about one of the business ideas!

JERICHA

Exactly. And then once he's ejaculated, he can just pop to the gents, or ask the cleaner or a new intern to rinse it out.

JOAN

Because otherwise I imagine it will get quite stinky? But there's nothing to say he can't use it two or three times before rinsing out?

JERICHA

Yes, I mean older guys will just be releasing a small sorry blob, so it won't fill so quickly. But with younger guys, there will of course be copious amounts.

JOAN

And for these elderly guys at home, they can also just clip it on inside their PJs, can't they?

JERICHA

Yes, there's one called the 'Cosypuss', based on those animal-style hot-water bottles with the hugging koala, or whatever.

JOAN

So it's hugging your penis?

JERICHA

That's it, because these older guys have lost that violent sex drive and want more of a snuggly sex pump.

JOAN

And I know the Riding Puss vulva comes in a range of pretty pinks, right up to the darker post-menopausal range.

JERICHA

Yes, the dark, ruddy, beefy shades – and even up to just a grey, shrivelled version ...

JOAN
The 'Gran Puss', yes. And that's
just an old bag with some—

JERICHA
Squirrel fur, Joan, yes.

The RIDING PUSS.
Private Penile Pleasure for Guys on the Go!

Chapter 6

WHY YOU'RE MENTALLY ILL

And Other Reasons He Hates You

It's very trendy nowadays to claim to be mentally ill. And we're seeing particularly the more self-obsessed ladies out there starting to hop on this bandwagon as a way to avoid all sorts of responsibilities, from not putting the bins out to refusing anal intercourse.

No longer are the divorced, dying or bereaved to be pitied – apparently, discovering that your favourite biscuit is unavailable in Waitrose, or your Starbucks coffee has two more bubbles in the froth than you'd hoped for, means you've been 'triggered' and this is your licence to start lashing out at hubby with sassy backchat, surly looks and foul-smelling wind, throughout the car ride home. Once through the door you announce you're going to bed with your antidepressants and a jeroboam of Baileys, leaving poor hubby without dinner or his usual early-evening manual release. This behaviour is not OK and could point to a very serious underlying condition like all over body cancer, or the rumblings of a serial killer eager to strike.

So Am I Crazy?

Sometimes ladies are not sure if they have mental health issues or not and it will often take a spouse to gently point it out. For extra confirmation, why not take our Harley Street certified quiz! (It's probably wise to get hubby to help – he can even play along and take it too!)

1) You go for dinner with your friend and she doesn't compliment you on your new haircut. Do you:

A) Strike her;
B) Start crying about all the ways you've been hurt in your life;
C) Insult her hair and face;
D) Stab yourself with the steak knife;
E) Tell her you're really happy with your new haircut.

2) Your mother buys you some pants as a birthday gift but they are two sizes too big. Do you:

A) Strike her;
B) Tell her you hate her, pull down her trousers and laugh at her vagina;
C) Go to the kitchen and gorge on fatty foods;
D) Try to slash your wrists;
E) Thank her, but explain you will exchange them for the right size in a sexier style.

3) You're spending Christmas at your boyfriend's parents and you ask your boyfriend if you look fat in your new jeans. He says 'not really'. Do you:

A) Strike him;

B) Tell him he looks fat and pointless and it's over;
C) Ask his dad if you're fat and give him a blow job if he says you're not;
D) Try and hang yourself near the Christmas tree;
E) Kiss your boyfriend and tell him you think you look really great in your new jeans.

RESULTS:
Mostly As (men): You're so good at feeling and expressing your anger. Good for you, it's really attractive!
Mostly As (women): You need to be sectioned.

Mostly Bs (men): You really keep people on their toes. Sexy!
Mostly Bs (women): You have a very self-pitying and spiteful streak. No wonder you're single!

Mostly Cs (men): This beautiful sensitivity must mean you're an amazing singer or actor.
Mostly Cs (women): You're very weird and unlikeable. You probably smell as well.

Mostly Ds (men): This martyred behaviour is almost saintly and you probably look like a surfer Jesus. You must work in a caring profession, but you're manly too. It's such a hot combo.
Mostly Ds (women): You're the type who always threatens suicide but never goes through with it. Why don't you do everyone a favour and do one thing in your life properly!

Mostly Es (men): You must be gay. Which is great! If not, you're adorable but you should try and have sex with more girls and then dump them in a really humiliating way – it will make you feel amazing!

Mostly Es (women): You're very stable. But, boy, are you boring! Try and do something to make yourself stand out a bit, like self-harming.

TRIGGERING TIMES

From this quiz, hubby will now have a correct medical diagnosis of your mental health status and be able to either pop you in a straitjacket, or shout at you to buck your ideas up and stop wasting everyone's time – like so many of these grim fakers who use super public holidays like Christmas to pretend to hear voices as a way of getting out of cooking, buying any decent presents or giving hubby his well-deserved Christmas Morn BJ!

JOAN
Honestly! I love Crimbo – with all the mini mince pies and slutty Santa lingerie!

JERICHA
Yes, and I know you always wear just your hooker heels and the fluffy thong for the family Christmas breakfast?

JOAN
Yes! With my sexy Santa hat!

JERICHA
But right now, you're in another fun hat for this chat about mental illness, Joan?

JOAN
Yes! This is a full English breakfast knitted beret, with a big brown sausage and lots of dangly bacon, made by Kerry Donglitt from Chippenham, whose husband very sadly took his own life last Boxing Day.

JERICHA
Awwww, well, Boxing Day can be quite a downer for some folk, Joan.

JOAN

Absolutely. I suppose all the prezzies are gone, and you've got trapped wind from gobbling too much turkey!

JERICHA

Indeed. Joking aside, though, suicide is common around this time of year and something you're sadly familiar with, Joan? As your first husband Noland, am I right, shot himself in the bath …

JOAN

… face, yes.

JERICHA

Oh, dear.

JOAN

We found his eyes still stuck to the shower curtain a week later.

JERICHA

As if he was still watching you?

JOAN

Yes, we couldn't get them off, so in the end we had to dispose of the shower curtain. Which was a shame because it was a very nice one from Zara Home, quite pricey …

JERICHA

What a nuisance. But did you feel Noland's act meant you'd failed in some way?

JOAN

No. He'd written lots of these awful finger-pointing notes, like, 'I hate you, Joan, you did this to me, you Scottish bitch, this is your fault and no one else's' and so on.

JERICHA

I suppose we'll never know who was to blame ...

Insecure Men

We all know that it's predominantly ladies who tend to be the ones with most of the problems 'upstairs', but occasionally things go wrong for some of these poor guys too. Joan opens up about her own, intimate story ...

JOAN: In the case of Noland, someone who started out as a fun, frothy kinda fella, dazzling me with his spicy bhunas and close-up magic, turned out, once we got married, to be a very different beast. Maybe I should have realised, a man who could magic a rabbit out of a hat, or yank a 6-foot-long hanky from his nostril might be hiding other things ...

Noland was profoundly bald when we first met, which he claimed happened falling out of a tree in his youth, but I think he'd copied that story from the sexy bald swimmer Duncan Goodhew. At first, I was able to overlook Noland's full-body hairlessness because of his big fat willy, which looked even bigger without hair – but bear in mind, this was the eighties, around the time of Whitesnake and Def Leppard and as a glamourpuss globe-trotting journalist, I got to interview these sex-on-legs guys with their bulgy leather trews and big, Bonnie Tyler hairdos. I would often dance for the guys on their tour bus and helped m'self to dozens of expensive snacks and tiny burgers, before and after gigs. Inevitably, Noland got insecure.

We were living in Kent at the time, in a huge mock-Tudor mansion with a fountain, a revolving patio, three heated pools and a paddock fit for twelve horses (although we didn't have any) so Noland kept all his wands and mirrors in the stables. After our first year there, trying for a baby every night, David Coverdale (lead singer of Whitesnake) moved in next door, with his morbidly obese wife, Jilly, who'd ballooned after a stage-diving incident went wrong. David and I used to do aerobics together most days, and he was always popping round to have a bounce on my trampoline, or to borrow a headband.

One Sunday it all came to a nasty head, when Noland caught me snogging David at his regular Sunday barbecue. We'd had several bottles of David's favourite pink Prosecco (and he was a pretty randy guy even after a cappuccino), so there he was flicking his frosted tips all over my boobs and thrusting his bunched-up leather crotch against mine, and I can't deny, I loved it. David's actual penis was very thin, but as the tip was so big, it unfortunately escaped above his waistband during our frenzied groin bashing and he ended up ejaculating a hefty jet, hitting poor Noland's mum (an elderly Whitesnake fan who was thrilled to have been invited to such an exclusive event) straight in the eye as she went in for a second sausage.

Noland went red with rage and burst into tears, thrusting his head onto the griddle in an attempt to burn his own face off, so distraught was he. David was furious because it was a new barbecue set and he ended up squirting mustard on Noland's bald head in a vengeful rage. Noland's mum was rushed to hospital but lost her sight in the sperm-battered eye, and I think that was what finally tipped Noland over the edge and into the tragic bathroom incident.

Truth is, some guys really feel they'd be more of a man if only they had a full head of hair. Noland might still be here today if an effective hair replacement product had been readily available on the market at a reasonable price. That's why, in his memory, I invented:

JOAN'S BALD-2-BUSH!

With Bald-2-Bush you can wave goodbye to tell-tale toupees and scalp-colouring-in pens, and say hello to a big healthy bush of fun 'n' fuzzy head hair!

Professional transplants can be very pricey, but with the Bald-2-Bush home kit you can harvest your own hair by snipping off a hefty strip of scrotal skin and tweezing those short and curlies into your empty head follicles. Those vacant scalp-holes just love a big juicy pubic hair shaft and will suck in those wiry wizards like a vacuum after crumbs. Within a week your scabs will be almost gone and you'll have a headstart with your fun 'n' fuzzy new look!

So go, enjoy showing off your growing helmet – and watch the ladies flock!

Disclaimer: your scrotal sac will be left misshapen with permanent denting and 89 per cent less fertility.

Loony Ladies

Clearly Noland's death was no one's fault, baldness being the baddy there, but for the majority of you, a depressed, upset or suicidal husband is always the result of the continued failings of an inattentive wife. So why is it that ladies are generally so difficult and mentally unstable?

Freud, of course, was fascinated by the anxious female mind, convinced that the main cause was the lady's frustrated, secret desire to have a penis of her own. This meant she would seek out private sexual satisfaction, often violently relieving herself with the frantic shovelling in and out of a Victorian mop handle, snaffled into her bedroom late at night. But the resulting build-up of fake satisfied libido from her frenzied wooden intercourse would take on a toxic character, finding its outlet in anxiety and, at worst, 'Hysteria' – Freud's (still very solid) theory that the womb itself is not tethered and therefore floats about the lady's body at random, causing her to become hot, flustered and unreasonable.

Certainly Mahmoud has seen this when performing his wonderful hysterectomies and in one case spent two hours trying to locate a lady's womb, only to discover it was actually lodged in her throat. Instead of removing it surgically via her vaginal vestibule, he had to feed her an out-of-date sandwich, causing her to vomit her womb out into a nearby kidney dish!

FEMALE PLEASURE

It is even more common nowadays for ladies to masturbate than in Victorian times, with the claim that it keeps them 'sane' – and many can be quite brazen in the DIY bedroom department. On top of expecting all kinds of pleasuring to her stinky from the man's penis, fingers or tongue, she can also be found hoarding a wild range of 'toys', both homemade and shop-bought, to go at herself with as the nights draw in. This type of lurid behaviour has echoes of Freud's lunatic lasses pumping away at themselves with brooms and pipes – and such ladies then quite rightly found themselves locked away in the asylums, something we would do well to reinstate today.

That said, we do offer booklets on what one should expect from hubby to achieve satisfaction below stairs (though he's certainly not obliged), and generally speaking one big lick and a meaty burp to vibrate the clitoris should do the trick once a year to ensure a balanced mind.

Our close work with Mahmoud and Dr Nupp has exposed the vital link between the clitoris and mental illness, with clinical findings revealing that the clitoris has a root that goes deep into the body, wraps around the spinal column like a Twister ice cream, helter-skelters up to the brain stem and then back down to the tummy button. If this is mildly inflamed through sexual pleasure it can be healthy, but too much stimulation can be most damaging, causing the type of mentally ill behaviour we see in ladies today.*

Having visited too many institutions with well-known TV presenters and royal friends drugged and deranged in rocking chairs, sporting designer straitjackets and Gucci electric shock hats, having suffered with their own tragic clitoral escapades, we felt compelled to share our most intimate tales ...

JOAN: Ralph's tiny toothy mouth and parroty tongue left me continually dissatisfied below and Mahmoud tried for many years to biggen Ralph's oral cavity, using his bangle-stretching technique so that I could experience more satisfying cunnilingus – but it just never took.

I knew Mahmoud was desperate to show Ralph how to do it himself, using his own bouncy mochaccino lips and moist, intelligent tongue. I've always had that 'will they won't they' chemistry with him and I can't deny there have been many times when I've ached for his big hot mouth on my large open vulva.

---

* If you are a celebrity then inevitably you are something of a cut above the rest and consequently can demand a little bit more in all areas of life, including when it comes to having your uglies eaten by the opposite sex, or partaking in intimate online-purchase-based self-pleasuring.

Mahmoud confirmed my clitoral root is deeper than any he's ever seen, with a stem as long as two trips around the world and back. So it's little wonder I've had to take lovers along the way and I've always been drawn to that Mick Jagger kind of mouth, with his floppy wet lips and a tongue down to his knees. In truth I did spend a night with Mick when he got separated from the other Stones on the Isle of Wight before a gig in the summer of 2000, having insisted he have a go on the donkey rides. I found him moping on the beach in his soiled flip-flops, very weepy, unable to locate his haggard colleagues, and most uncomfortable in his tight sweaty trousers. We shared a giant creamy carbonara in Zizzi's that evening and then got Danny,* my sexy security guy, to drop us back to my hotel as Mick had lost his Haven Hall room key. I was at the Ibis, so it was frankly like a squat as far as Mick was concerned, and he kicked up quite a stink. I helped him off with his sticky drainpipes and gave him a quick bed bath (as he'd spilt an awful lot of his carbonara into his pants), and then went about pleasuring him with one of my Killer Blowies. But he must have been too full from his creamy pasta as he dozed off midway through, and proceeded to fart freely throughout the night.

In the morning, I was up early to freshen up my downstairs in preparation for a hearty round of Mickilingus, but when I emerged from the bathroom, freshly shaved below, he'd scarpered, having stolen the complimentary Shrewsbury biscuits and my new Next shower cap!

JERICHA: Poor Joan, a tragic tale indeed and one Mick devotes a paragraph to in his autobiography *Taking The Mick*. But I too have suffered a lack of oral attention on the ground floor due to Phillip spending the bulk of his time tending to his Thai Scout teens. Even on our honeymoon, Phillip, though eager to 'gobble up my little

* See Appendix B.

kitty', as I murmured to him when the lights were low, ended up vomiting onto it when he got down there. Admittedly, I was holding his head pretty firmly and bobbing it up and down forcefully, having got rather carried away after a good deal of sangria, but from that point onwards he said he could only associate my lower concourse with extreme nausea.

We tried various techniques to desensitise him, the most successful being when I donned a jokey pair of pants a male friend had given him with a photo of an erect penis spouting semen printed on the front. Phillip felt able to put his mouth on the outside of the pants and lick the fabric, which did bring me to immediate climax, but then, poor thing, the sickness overcame him again. Ironically, poor Dr Nupp had similar issues with me when we were briefly dating before I met Phillip. His long penis was perfectly pleasant up my lengthy vestibule, but when it came to burrowing his tongue 'down there', he got rather shy.

Luckily Mahmoud furnished me, for purely medical reasons, with an emergency 'Meaty Licks' session that he developed with Dr Nupp – much like the Masters and Johnson research team of the 1950s – and I must say it was one of the most glorious afternoons I have ever spent. It put me in a place of deep relaxation for over a year.

WOMEN WHO GET TOO BIG FOR THEIR BOOTS

Sometimes, women do start to overthink things, rather than focusing on the needs of their husbands and children. This is an illness in itself (and very unfeminine). They start questioning the man they are living with and somehow feel they could do better. Sometimes they will even *pretend* to be mentally ill in order to strike out solo, saying they 'need space' when in fact they are secretly planning a five-year bonkathon, hoping to catch up on sampling every size, shape and colour of penis they've missed out on during their 'dull' married years riding hubby's weary winky.

Ninety-nine times out of a hundred, however, they'll end up as ghastly single mums who nobody wants to invite for dinner. Because, like the Prowling Spinster, Ms Single Mum'll come slinking round your kitchen, guzzling rosé, dressed in some boob-boasting, vulva-skimming scrap of chiffon she claims is a dress, keeping her mouth wide open throughout dinner in case of any passing guest penises. That, or she arrives without a bottle and brings the whole group down with her weepy wine talk about her ghastly, lonely life and difficult children. She'll blackmail you into taking her on one of your functional family's holidays, then spend the whole time topless, pointing her boobs at your husband in the hope of some action, but with nothing doing, hoick her shaved puddy round the village at midnight, and haul back a swarthy local to bonk all night on the diving board. One to avoid at all costs.

DEPRESSED PIGGY LADIES

Some women use their difficulties with mental imbalance as an excuse to gorge themselves stupid, and many find themselves descending into a vicious spiral of frantic fatty snackings to boost their mood – but then end up loathing themselves because they can no longer squeeze their bulky behinds into their wet-look, speed-dating jeggings!

JOAN
Obviously, a lot of ladies find it hard to control
their appetites, Jericha, blaming it on manic
depression. But is it ever OK to get tubby-
tummed or crumpet-thighed?

JERICHA
No! It's ghastly, Joan, not only will you look
dreadful, but that slothful piggery will drastically
and in some cases irreversibly, lower your mood.
So exercise has never been more important.

JOAN

Now of course your go-to is 'wild swimming' in Regent's Canal – or indeed any body of water you have access to. But if water weren't available, how would you exercise?

JERICHA

Well, one can always pretend-swim on a carpet, something I do if the canal is being dredged, for example, as there are frequently body parts drifting by on my morning swim.

JOAN

How many lengths would you do on the carpet?

JERICHA

At least sixty, Joan. But other mood boosters for me are big-stride jogging and, of course, tennis! I'm a bit of a tennis nut, and I'm not ashamed to say I have been all sorts of shapes and sizes in my life, but it didn't affect my game one jot, because I don't tend to move about the court much anyway.

JOAN

Yes, some readers may not know that you have very long arms which gives you enormous reach on the court.

JERICHA

Yes, it's a condition Joan, bracchium vulgaris, meaning they're about 50 per cent longer than a 'normal' person's arms.

JOAN

Goodness, well I know Michael Fassbender has very long arms.

JERICHA

And a very long penis.

JOAN

Very long. I saw that film *Shame* and honestly it was skimming his knees.

JERICHA

Wonderful actor.

JOAN

Wonderful penis. He just oozes, doesn't he? But I mean almost any Irish man would have my knickers down in seconds.

JERICHA

Well, it's that lilt, Joan, isn't it? The twinkly eye, the warm brogue.

JOAN

And the stories ... I mean Dave Allen, gorgeous ... and Liam Neeson.

JERICHA

Also hugely blessed down below.

JOAN

Graham Norton ...

JERICHA

Obviously, he's gay.

JOAN
But he's Irish and as far as I know packs quite a punch in his trousers.

GET IN SHAPE! WITH JERICHA'S MOOD-BOOSTING CANAL WORKOUT

I've always adored cold water. Even as a child I would plead with Mother, a much-feared heavyweight boxer who once slayed a Russian man with her One Finger Punch, to let me join her in her ice baths after a big fight. I longed to share in what looked, through the keyhole, like ecstasy, as I spied her wrestling her long-necked rubber ducks between her huge pumping thighs, growling with pleasure and then snapping their heads off as her violent shuddering subsided. Occasionally she would allow me to bring her dinner and sit on the edge of the bath as she gorged on a lamb carcass, wool and all.

As the years have gone by, however, I have unfortunately developed a circulation issue, meaning that now when I take my dawn plunge into Regent's Canal, my fingers darken and my nose purples and swells, often to the size of an average aubergine. This can be awkward if I'm due to do a telly appearance. My wonderful make-up artist Mandy can improve the colour with a hefty dollop of foundation, but size-wise, it persists in blocking most of my other features and I've often heard people laughing at me behind the cameras.

Even more profound has been a blackened and over-sensitive pudenda, or *mons major*, which is why I have had to keep that area well covered with my pubic ebullience. In fact, at times I allowed it to grow so freely, I had essentially developed a full pair of hairy-pants. Sadly that dense bush has worn away with my advancing years, the baldening made worse by all the mini hot-water bottles and tiny blankets sent in by well-wishers – including a crotcheted mini doormat, from a fat man in Deal, who asked if I could send him a video of me rubbing it on my *mons major* til I climaxed. Needless to say I declined.

I find my lengthy swims to be an invaluable mood booster, taking my daily route from the Maida Hill Tunnel to Limehouse where I do my 'PUMP IT!' canal and towpath workout routine, often to a gathered, though uninvited, crowd which seems to lift their moods, as well as my own.

PUMP IT!

PUMP IT! is a combination of dirty dancing, pelvic-pumping and violent underwater boxing – bashing fishes and discarded plimsolls out of the way as you tone your way to success.

I was first taught PUMP IT! by the leader of a synchronised swimming team I joined when I was living in an all-ladies house in High Wycombe, after the sudden death of my first husband Randy. 'Nose-Peg Jill', as she became known, was a legend in the synchro world (now sadly dead having been mowed down by a stag weekend boat, and trapped beneath screaming, throughout their entire weekend of revelries). Luckily I was able to retrieve Jill's nose, slightly scuffed, but complete with peg, and I keep that displayed in a pretty glass box on my hallway wall. It's always a wonderful icebreaker!

I often credit Nose-Peg Jill's routine with boosting my mood and thereby maintaining my wonderful marriage. And when Joan's husband Ralph is compos mentis, she often tips him out of his wheelchair (with the help of her muscly French live-in chef and exercise guru, Pierre*) into the moat surrounding her castle, screaming directions at him, based on this routine, in an attempt to reactivate his dead muscle tissue.

---

* See Appendix B.

EXERCISE A:

MONS THRUST.

(This is marvellous for the hip joints and gives the clitoris a mini massage, which will always lift a low mood.)

EXERCISE B:

BOTTY BUMPS.

(For the perfect Kardashian bottyshelf. Big round bottoms are attractive and fun so whack your booty against the concrete canal sides and watch it swell!)

EXERCISE C:

VULVIC PUMPIES.

(This involves puffing air in and out of the vaginal vestibule and the more advanced amongst us can even play a tune from our vulvas.)

EXERCISE D:

FLATTY TUM TUM.

(Use a heavy implement or some floating driftwood to bash your flabby tum flat, and don't worry if there is substantial bleeding.)

EXERCISE E:

BOOB PLUMP.

(This incorporates a shimmying of the breasts, much as you would see from a tarty lady in a strip club jiggling her nipple tassels, followed by my Seagull Wing Spreader, which builds the pectoral muscles thus thrusting your boobs forward.)

EXERCISE F:

THIGH GAP CHALLENGE.

(Carry a scaffolding pole between your legs for the entire nine-mile swim.)

DEPRESSIVE MARKERS

JOAN

Jericha, as many folk will know, you've written several books on depression.

JERICHA

Yes, five books in total.

JOAN

All of which are very similar?

JERICHA

Yes, they're pretty much a republishing of each book, Joan, with a little tweak here and there.

JOAN

Usually just a couple of sentences.

JERICHA

Only needs to be.

JOAN

Absolutely. Now I know people often ask you if you ever feel that Cardinal's depression might be your fault, given that you ignored her until she was five.

JERICHA

Yes, and then off she went to boarding school. But no, I feel I've been a wonderfully devoted mother and with a head that size, we all knew something was profoundly wrong with her from the get-go.

JOAN

No doubt about that. And I believe Mahmoud created a test that shows up these depressive markers in her blood and what its origins were?

JERICHA

Yes, so we have established in Cardinal's case that it's from her father's side – not Phillip, but her real father, who you've always said, Joan, looked remarkably like Fred West.

JOAN

Yes, although we're not necessarily saying it actually was him?

JERICHA

Not necessarily, no.

JOAN

But what's fab with a test like this is it means you're able to ... not exactly *blame* someone else, but be able to say to them, 'This is all your fault.'

JERICHA

Exactly. You know, 'I'm a great mum, I'm innocent, so this is all your problem.'

JOAN

Very comforting. Now, I know you have a yummy recipe to share that Phillip introduced you to, which can help with the more down-in-the-dumpsy, moany types who need a boost of serotonin?

JERICHA

Yes! These are Phillip's fatty balls or 'Phillip's fat balls', which are so yummy and easy to make. I call them nature's antidepressants – and often secretly crumble them up into Cardinal's cornflakes!

PHILLIP'S FATTY BALLS

Phillip first introduced me to his Fatty Balls when we began dating, as something to nibble on during our romantic excursions, which were usually outdoor assault courses of one kind or another. He was very much the Bear Grylls of his time, yomping about in cargo shorts and bulky butterscotch Timberland's and our dates were these fun endurance activities, where he would air-drop me into the middle of huge dark woods to fend for myself, whilst he helped little local boys to construct huts, stripped to their pants to build resilience, but with plenty of alcohol to keep them warm! And so, when he finally came for me after a few days, I'd be ravenous to gobble on his big greasy balls, having survived on potentially poisonous berries and infected rodents.

He'd first got the recipe from his mother, a very striking woman, with more than a hint of Mark Bolan, who could often be seen cramming two or more fatty balls into her mouth at any given time.

METHOD

You'll need to gather fat from as many sources as possible: bacon, ham, steak, pork but also do check in restaurant bins, as they often have piles of solidified fat there that will be perfect to mould. And don't be afraid to snaffle some bits from the dog's bowl if necessary, or have a little rummage down your plug hole.

I'm not a fan of kitchen utensils per se, so I tend to use my teeth whenever I can and certainly to tear off these greasy fat chunks – and my very acidic saliva helps to bind the bits together. I then drill a hole into an everyday ping-pong ball and blow the fatty bits in using a straw, until the ball is full.

I always do a big batch of them on a Sunday evening and pop them in the freezer – then whenever I feel nibbly or a bit low I take one out, snip open the ping-pong ball and gobble down on the fatty sphere.

Wonderful to wipe around your gums when undergoing a mood swing, these will also freshen up a pongy mouth, as mentally ill people often smell like they've been feasting on dog poo.

When Ladies Blame Men

It's a simple law of nature that sometimes guys are driven to strike ladies, but nowadays it's become fashionable for disgruntled wives to refer to this type of energetic swiping as 'domestic violence', and exaggerate the normal horseplay that goes on in all marital homes. Often this is because she's secretly angling for a mini-break at a bed and breakfast or some kind of extra pocket money from the government, to fritter on bras and biscuits. The key here, ladies, is to look to yourselves and ask: hang on a minute! What was my part in this? How did I cause poor hubby to lash out? What can I do better next time?

JOAN

'Dear Joan and Jericha, my husband Frank drinks three bottles of wine each evening and often becomes aggressive. I have found hidden bottles of alcohol around the house and even caught him drinking my perfume. My friend

says he's an alcoholic, but when I mentioned this to him, he swung at me with a golf club. Is my friend right? Or am I being paranoid?'
Ruth Flan, from Dorset

JERICHA
Hello, Ruth, thanks for writing in, albeit with a rather finger-pointy letter.

JOAN
Gosh, this is a tricky one really, hard to tell, isn't it?

JERICHA
Yes, because look, a lot of men enjoy a drink and why shouldn't they? They work bloody hard ... so three bottles an evening, was it?

JOAN
Yes, and the perfume, of course.

JERICHA
Well, the perfume's another matter, Joan, he may well have simply had a nasty taste in his mouth and thought a bit of a swill would give his oral area a freshen up.

JOAN
Yes, because of his boozy breath. Or Ruth could well have been bullying him about an ongoing halitosis issue.

JERICHA
Wouldn't surprise me, Joan, looking at her photo. And OK, I think if he was drinking seven or eight bottles of perfume a day ...

JOAN

Is that the number where you'd start to worry?

JERICHA

Yes, you would have alarm bells ringing, Joan, if you had a whole range of perfumes and suddenly you wake up and they're all gone from your dressing table.

JOAN

Well it's annoying when they're so pricey. But looking at Ruth Flan's photo, she's not striking me as a woman with expensive perfumes.

JERICHA

No, she's more of a Body Shop White Musk or Charlie Red type. You know, these cheap old, studenty ones, and it looks to me rather like she's hung on to these ancient perfumes, not updating them as she herself ages.

JOAN

Yes. So she's poisoning poor old Frank Flan by making him drink these nasty old congealed perfumes.

JERICHA

And it really does beg the bigger question, why is Frank Flan being driven to drink your perfumes in the first place, Ruth?

JOAN

Well, she doesn't look like a woman who can cook, and many perfumes contain important nutrients. So it may well be that Frank is simply hungry.

JERICHA

Yes, he'd be getting some vitamins C and E, Joan – and very nice skin if he's drinking, for example, a rose-based perfume.

JOAN

Also good for enbiggening breasts, is rose. It can take you up three cup sizes.

JERICHA

Well, look, Frank may well be after some moobs. Perhaps he's trying to stop himself having an affair by growing his own breasts to fondle. Certainly Ruth's don't look much cop.

JOAN

No. They're more like a pair of old flaps. And what about this 'he swung at me with a golf club' business?

JERICHA

She doesn't say where he swung at her, because if she was standing in his way on the golf course, then it's her fault.

JOAN

No, in her longer letter she says she was in the kitchen eating her breakfast and he whacked her with it about her trunk, with a big bonk on her head for good measure.

JERICHA

Poor guy probably just trying to practise his swing, Joan, you see these guys at it in offices all the time. And if not, Ruth needs to ask herself, 'OK, if it was deliberate, how have I brought my husband to a place where he needs to strike me?'

JOAN

If you actually look at Ruth Flan's photo there, she's very pudgy, very ruddy, with that big strawberry purple nose ...

JERICHA

Ghastly! Joan, I'd like to strike her myself.

JOAN

Me too, but what I'm wondering is ... possibly, this is not what it seems?

JERICHA

Indeed, it could be that Ruth Flan is herself a bitter alcoholic lady – we see this quite a lot don't we, Joan, unhappy ladies projecting all their nasty behaviours on to hubby?

JOAN

I'm sick to death of it, really.

JERICHA

And poor Frank Flan ... what a lovely name, like a poem.

JOAN

Frank Flan, the jolly old man.

JERICHA

Spent his life in a caravan ...

JOAN

And that is what you will be doing, Ruth Flan, if you're not careful.

Shortly after receiving this letter we understand Ruth Flan passed away, having been found in several pieces in a wood, a golf club by her side. This only confirms our theory that this raspberry-nosed harlot was lashing out at poor Frank, projecting her problems on to him and either bonked herself to death with his golf club or paid some well-meaning friend to do so and then chop her up in an attempt to frame poor Frank.

Luckily Frank Flan has been able to provide a watertight alibi: he was at a Masons' charity meeting on the night in question and had several local police officers and former DJs to vouch for his innocence, poor guy. Fortunately he has now managed to pick up the pieces and has impregnated a number of local ladies as well as improving his handicap at golf, so big congrats to Frank and the very best of wishes.

Sadly, all too often we get letters like this from women who are trying to paint the picture of themselves as the victim, rather than the unbalanced catalyst of all their marital ills, trying to manipulate us into calling on one of the many attractive policemen we know around Britain in the hope they will visit her for a flirty cup of tea and some furtive fumblings, maybe an evening out at a long-running musical, whilst one of the bulky lesbian police ladies carts hubby off for a night in the cells whilst she attempts to sexually assault a happily married bobby. It won't wash, so please don't send these in. It's your own time you're wasting.

Chapter 7

WHY YOU DROVE HIM TO DIVORCE YOU

When Single Mums Become Toxic Tarts

A lot of these unstable and downright difficult ladies end up driving poor hubby to have to divorce them. Dumped and dowdy, these desperate lasses then commence a rabid mission to ensnare a new fella, but having hawked their battered wares all over the internet and failed, they end up venting all their frustrations on their children. And if they do miraculously trap some poor unsuspecting chap, they make a right royal hash of things by displaying jealous and accusatory behaviour, particularly towards their pubescent daughters ...

JOAN

'Dear Joan and Jericha, I've been divorced five years and recently met a lovely fella at my local church and we've been enjoying day trips to the sea and stately homes and some really nice sex. He gets on really well with my daughter and recently said he's attracted to her. I got very upset and he said I was being nasty and jealous and paranoid, so I apologised. That evening I went to my garage to get a tub of mint ice cream from my chest freezer and found them doing it doggy style on the concrete floor. What should I do?' Denise Bent, Cumberland

JERICHA

Oh goodness, Denise. It's exhausting really this, isn't it, Joan. We seem to get the same sort of letters from these rather, I don't know, what's the word?

JOAN

Well, jealous, sort of bitter, nasty ladies.

JERICHA

Indeed. And I don't know who keeps chest freezers in garages any more?

JOAN

Apart from serial killers!

JERICHA

Exactly.

JOAN

So, she's divorced, this Denise Bent, she's been round the block and back and now she's snaffled this guy at church by pretending to be a Christian, which I really don't think she is.

JERICHA

Doesn't look like one.

JOAN

Not with that mouth, no. In her longer letter, she says they've had these days out to stately homes where Martin's paid for all the nice baguettes and lemon drizzle cakes she's been having, and buying her gifts in the gift shop – whatever she wants ...

JERICHA

And they're not cheap those baguettes, are they, Joan?

JOAN

No.

JERICHA

Even a pot of tea is quite pricey, and you add on the cost of lemon drizzle and a clutch of knick-knacks from the gift shop.

JOAN

Absolutely. And Martin's prepared to pay and carry the tray and so on. And now Denise has got the hump that he's shown some affection for her daughter!

JERICHA

I mean, he's clearly a genuine
churchgoer, this Martin, he's a
fine upright fellow, and that's a
lovely picture of him, isn't it, on
that monocycle – goodness that's
a skill!

JOAN

Very unusual.

JERICHA

Yes, he looks like a fun sort of a
fella, albeit with a bit of a tum
there that might unbalance him
on that.

JOAN

I'm actually amazed he can stay
on because that tum's spilling
right down, isn't it, towards
the wheel?

JERICHA

Absolutely, but he's obviously a very fun
fellow to be around. I mean how old
is the daughter, does she say?

JOAN

She's just turned sixteen.

JERICHA

Yes, so he's lovely fun company for her and I
imagine he's taught her some basic circus skills
and then one thing's led to another, Joan, in
the garage by the chest freezer.

JOAN

Well, absolutely. Denise Bent sent some video footage of them doing it doggy style and of course with him being so big and tubby, she's shown his stomach slapping back and forth in slow motion.

JERICHA

Yes, it was quite a fun video in many ways, but obviously she was trying to point to it as evidence of his—

JOAN

I don't know, would you call it lechery perhaps, as a Christian?

JERICHA

In all honesty, though, it looks like a rather fun *It's A Knockout* type of event, with his great bumping, bulging ball of a tum and this fun energetic young lass with her little crop top and shorts, her hair in those bunches and the hefty false eyelashes – she's made the very best of quite a piggy face, Joan.

JOAN

Absolutely, and you can see why he's beside himself, it's all very Britney Spears, isn't it?

JERICHA

Before she was sectioned, yes, I mean it's what girls do, I'm afraid, and what fella, this lovely devout man included, can resist?

JOAN

I think what's tricky is that Denise Bent has tried to ape the same look in this photo she's enclosed of herself masturbating, with her withered grey bunches and the school uniform, but the nipples are drooping out well belowthe crop top, actually skimming her waistband – and it's just not working on a woman of forty-plus!

JERICHA

No, not with a skin condition like that, Joan, this sort of crocodiley texture to the skin and a greenish hue. Looks to me like a condition known as 'crocodile psoriasis', which does need immediate attention from a GP.

JOAN

Yes, I've seen this before, where the face starts to take on not just the texture, but the crocodilian shape, with that rather lengthy nose and jaw.

JERICHA

Yes, she does have the heavily protruding snout and the bulgy eyes.

JOAN

And look, she's actually enclosed another picture of herself in the bath there, with just the bulging eyes poking out above the water …

JERICHA

This condition is usually viral, Joan. She will have picked it up from rolling around

on dirty ground – perhaps in the churchyard
after the service where people have been
recently interred.

JOAN

So there's all sorts of reasons here why Martin
would rather be intercoursing a sexy schoolgirl
than an ageing crocodile.

JERICHA

Mm ... I've actually got some other alarm bells
ringing, Joan, about Denise Bent's ex-husband
and that chest freezer. I'm just wondering
if she caught this crocodile virus and went for
him, then whisked his body parts into a mint
ice cream which she's kept in the chest freezer,
and then told everyone he'd left her?

JOAN

That does sound like the most likely
explanation, yes, and it looks like poor Martin
could be next!

JERICHA

Let's hope he gets away on his unicycle!

DUMBO PENIS

But how does single mum status affect boys? Well, we are seeing a strange phenomenon on the rise, whereby the son's penis begins to grow wildly out of control once Dad's out of the picture. Both Dr Nupp and Mahmoud have been studying these boys for many years (Phillip also tried to get involved but for some reason was banned), and neither diet nor hormones were found to be relevant to this uncontainable and boisterous penile biggening.

What seems most likely, according to their findings, is that in the absence of a father figure, the son unconsciously feels obliged to show Mum his manliness by developing a bigger and bigger member. This is known as the Dumbo Penis. Sometimes Dad will have had a substantial member himself – known as the Jumbo Penis (or the Daddy Jumbo) – but equally he may have been rather disappointing down there, and little Josh's sudden lengthening and phallic fattening can be an enormous surprise for Mum, when she first glimpses what she initially thinks is a new bath toy as he swishes it about in the water. But soon enough she will find Josh dragging his whopping willy about the house behind him, and during the night can hear its eerie scrape along the hallway carpet, as the sleepless boy paces his trailing trunk up and down until dawn.

Despite the worry, mums can feel privately very proud of sons with this condition, particularly when he can entice married mums from proper families to her usually sparse coffee mornings. Even snooty mums who didn't initially want to attend get wind of the lad's whopper and now arrive early, caked in make-up, wearing tight, clingy clothes, finding constant excuses to get Josh to stand up and walk about so they can get a decent ogle, often jiggling their boobs or plucking at their vulvas in his eyeline so that they can marvel at his resultant bulging trouser telescope.

Once summer comes, the lad can even pick up buns with it, or shower groups of people before they go into the outdoor swimming pool and little toddlers often want to hop on Josh's big party snake for a ride around the pool (as one would on the inflatable bananas in the sea, on a Greek holiday). Some of the more grabby mums will even charge for tickets.

Come puberty, some sons with the Dumbo go from the confident hunky stud that all the girls want a go on, to a growing sense that they are some kind of circus freak, as interested ladies begin to have understandable concerns about their vulvas exploding. Masturbation is, of course, a very hot potato for these chunky chaps and besides the fact that they black out after every ejaculation, the mere mechanics of attempting to stimulate this chubby canon with normal-sized hands is nigh on impossible.

Luckily Dr Nupp and Mahmoud have come up with some practical solutions!

THE DUMBO DAZZLER

The **Dumbo Dazzler** (originally designed for rogue elephants) with its snazzy, state-of-the-art, chrome-look giant hands and sexy lube nozzles, straps on to the base of your huge shaft and works its way up to your helmet and back down, whilst playing sexy music of your choice! With adjustable pressure and speed, the **Dazzler** will give you the ultimate 'hand shandy' and you can just lie back and enjoy!

Waterproof ceiling cover included.

... AND THE DUMBARROW

A wheelbarrow for your whopper. Sometimes you just want to wander about your garden in your birthday suit without having to trip over your big fella. With the **DumBarrow** you can wheel it around indoors or out, enjoying the breeze about your big boy and in between your buttocks, whilst keeping your dumbo penis free of floor-chafing and unsightly crumbs.

The **DumBarrow** comes in **Fireman Red**, **Berlin Black** and **Simply Spotty** – for fun guys who just want the world to smile!

OLDER SINGLE WOMEN

'But Joan and Jericha, what about us older single mums, who still want sex?!' we hear these old nuisances cry. The geriatric single mum who is eager to 'put it about a bit' may rightly harbour some niggling private concerns, namely that her vagina is rather baggy and worn out (it usually is), as like cheap socks the vagina does tend to bag and fray with excess use. (And that isn't simply sexual, it's often just walking about, getting wind up it and so forth.)

Frequently, surgery is unaffordable, as this brash bint has usually lost some embittered battle to rinse her husband of his hard-earned cash and has been fired from her job, being too unstable to hold a position of any authority with her haggard looks born of fatty takeaways and boozy nights trawling for men. So she then takes on a more lowly position in a local supermarket, but gets the heave-ho because of her constant attempts to flirt with male customers, asking if they need help with 'packing their bag' or offering up endless ideas for dinner, and unwanted recipe tips. In essence, she is a sex pest who has no money, no job and a big baggy vagina.

'SO HOW CAN I "PUT IT ABOUT"?'

There is one solution when surgery is out of the question and you really feel the need to foist your gnarly nethers around town. If you got lucky and have managed to force a drunk man home, quickly turn the lights off (unless he's blind, which he may well be), pull your pants down, lie on a nearby couch, turn yourself back to front and simply pretend your anus is your vagina.

The only issue may be confusion if he thinks your buttocks are some very big vaginal lips, but you can always splay them as much as possible (or use our portable botty-clamps) for your front to back switcheroo. If the blotto guy's doing oral and he's searching in vain for the clitoris, pop some Blu Tack just above your anus and he will happily rub away at it. Then you can make the appropriate sex noises, or use a porn recording, but you are in danger of the putty changing shape and falling off. Luckily, Mahmoud and Dr Nupp have created some super stick-on clitorises that you can pop just above your anus once the lights are out. These come in boxes of ten, in different shades, shapes and sizes. Simply stick on with superglue and enjoy!

Disclaimer: these don't come off, or if they do they will take with them a huge chunk of botty skin.

SHE-POOS

Another danger for the older and desperate divorcee, however, can be a ragged rear if she constantly passes off her anus for a vagina. And all too often these louche 'n' lusty ladies suffer with a big baggy botty. She will doubtless have already over-used her anus throughout her marriage – but rarely from pleasing hubby as she should have done, more often it's stretched from incorrect pushing during labour, eventually causing the whole thing to pop out like a bit of old hosepipe. Or, she may have trashed said anus through secretly gorging on too many pastries and sausage rolls throughout her marriage, often hiding the long Greggs ones inside her pillowcase to wolf on during the night and thus jamming her guts with pounds of white dough, creating appalling constipation – meaning her daily, fruitless strainings have flared the bowel to the point where it now billows like a wizard's sleeve, allowing stools to escape unannounced throughout the day.

But many of these greedy, now-single gals, truffling on take-aways and cheap Chardonnay night after night, are simply desperate for a guy to service them, to quell the rising panic that she made a dreadful mistake if she had the audacity to leave hubby of her own accord. So most Saturdays, she can be seen shimmying about her front room to Chaka Khan, in her tight leather skirt and cork-heeled wedges, glugging a large Martini, before tottering to her local bar to lure back some poor fella for a bout of boozy intercourse in her new bed with chunky foam topper. But how can she ride ruddy-faced Roger into next week, if she's concerned about releasing rogue stools?

JOAN
Well, Cardinal's She-Wees were a big hit, so
now these baggy-bottomed divorcees
are after the She-Poos.

JERICHA
Yes, Mahmoud has a super range online in
all the colours of the rainbow, but also in some
very classy, neutral shades so that no one will
know.

JOAN
There's a gorgeous rust brown, which I love for
autumn sex sessions and that also makes sense
because that's the colour of your faeces.

JERICHA
For the most part.

JOAN
And then pretty, coloured, flowery ones for
summer, with the sexy, lacy trims.

JERICHA
Wonderful. So, let's say you're about to make
love, but you're a bit jumbly below, you just
attach it to your anus, and then you can enjoy
some vibrant sexual intercourse whilst
quietly filling your She-Poo.

JOAN

And what's lovely is the She-Poo will just swing with you, as you move about during the sex act.

JERICHA

And if you fill it up completely, halfway through sex, you can distract your guy with something, and quickly snap it off, pop the heavied one in your handbag and clip on a fresh one.

JOAN

Yes, because I think most women carry a handbag during sex.

JERICHA

Oh, you always hang on to your handbag, don't you, Joan? Much as you would at a disco.

JOAN

Indeed. So, deciding what size of She-Poo you want is dependent on the size of your anus?

JERICHA

Yes, and the type of faeces you do: are you a rabbit dropping, segmented, pebbly kind of lady? Or more of a coiling snake, ranging right up to the giant elephant faeces that some of our ladies – these larger ladies, who are eating lots of meat – will require.

JOAN

And what type of perfume do you want your bespoke She-Poo pipe to smell of?

JERICHA

There's all sorts of fragrances, from spring onions through to orange blossom, white musk, and we've even got – and it might sound counter-intuitive, but it's a big turn-on for a lot of guys – 'faecal', if your faeces don't actually smell very much and you want to boost that side of things.

JOAN

Some guys do love the smell of really strong faeces.

JERICHA

Oh, guys just go bananas for it!

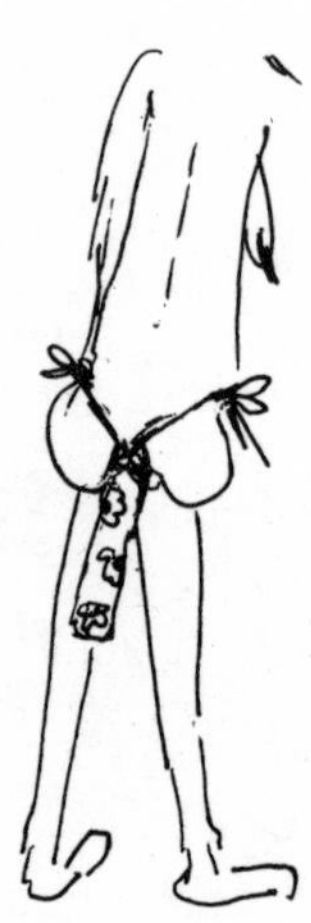

'SO CAN I MARRY MY DOG?'

Unfortunately for many ladies, they have to accept that having lost hubby, and despite all their best efforts, they will never again have anything human thrusting at their vaginas, apart from an angry practice nurse when she goes in for a hearty rummage with her cervical fork.

In most cases these poor lasses gallop to their graves depressed, heavily made up (often wearing an overly short skirt and low cut top, having insisted on an open casket), still on the lookout for some penile interest, even as their body lies cold and stiff! But what if Mr Right was right under their noses ... all along?!

JOAN

'Dear Joan and Jericha, I have had very little success with men and have reached the point where I'm wondering if I could marry my dog? Friends and family think I'm weird, but I have heard this is a "thing" and I do get on quite well with my dog. What do you think?' And that's from Sylvia Bomberoon, sixty-one, from Wiltshire.

JERICHA

Yes, well it's a funny old thing. isn't it, Joan? These dogs are such wonderful creatures, aren't they, with these wet nuzzly noses and misty eyes. Just so much to love, and so affectionate ...

JOAN

Indeed, and the particular dog Sylvia has is a pit bull crossed with a mastiff crossed with a german shepherd, so it's quite an aggressive dog. She describes it as very manly.

JERICHA

OK …

JOAN

She says she always used to go out with tough, burly guys who used a certain amount of – well, violence is a strong word, but I think she got herself into a few tussles and it's obviously what she likes. So she's not looking for a docile, dumpy Labrador – she wants something a lot more challenging.

JERICHA

So what's this dog called, do we know?

JOAN

He's called Griff.

JERICHA

Goodness, quite a gruff, manly sort of a name, isn't it?

JOAN

Yes, very sexy – and at sixty-one, Sylvia's been around the block and back really, she's been in these violent relationships up til now, and wants to get married but keeps picking Mr Wrong.

JERICHA

Yes, people talk about Mr Wrong, Joan, but very often it's Mrs Wrong or Ms Wrong, who's obviously not providing the right environment for a real man to want to step into her life. And it's no surprise really to hear, Joan, that the only mammal she's managed to get on with for this entire time is her pet dog Griff.

JOAN

Sadly, though, even with Griff it's tricky because she says he's very moody, he's very sulky, he'll turn on a sixpence ... So they'll be having a perfectly nice dinner together, they'll be watching an ITV vet programme – and suddenly he'll stalk off, out the room in a foul mood, do a pool of diarrhoea in the hall and go to bed!

JERICHA

Oh goodness, so it's not that far off some people's marriages, is it, Joan? I mean, the point here is this dog can't speak, presumably – unless she's managed to teach him some basic words?

JOAN

Well, she says he can. She's sent in some footage of what she believes is him speaking. She said he speaks two languages – I can't see it, but she's absolutely convinced.

JERICHA

It sounds to me like Sylvia has loaded a lot of expectations onto poor Griff, as you would an ideal man, and what's happening is that the dog is stressed. She's trying to teach him all these foreign languages and it's got to the point where the dog's had enough and stormed off.

And why shouldn't he? Sylvia Bomberoon's not only failed to meet the needs of all these men in her past, but is now no longer meeting the needs of this poor manly dog.

JOAN

She says that Griff goes out in the evenings and often has dinner with a woman, Belinda, who runs a nearby dress shop – and Sylvia says she'll go out in her dressing gown to post letters and look through the window to see Griff and this lady Belinda enjoying a candlelit cheese and biscuit supper. And she gets very jealous, she'll start hammering on the window and shouting at them – and I think Griff wants out, if I'm honest.

JERICHA

Well, we know dogs are very food driven and goodness, I mean if this Belinda lady at the dress shop's offering some upmarket cheese and biscuits – I mean, we don't know what else is on offer after the dinner, do we?

JOAN

No, and Sylvia says Belinda's always just in her bra and pants when she looks through the window at 11 o'clock at night.

JERICHA

Well, lucky old Griff! It sounds to me like he's got his priorities right, doesn't it? I mean, he'll have already eaten at Sylvia's house, probably a rather basic dog's dinner, so he's thinking, Well, hang on, I'm getting these after dinner treats and a bit of this and that – perhaps even a bit of the other, if Belinda's in her pretty lingerie set.

JOAN

And she sounds like a much nicer lady, doesn't she, Belinda, if she runs a dress shop – that shows a sort of flair and femininity.

JERICHA

Yes, these dress shop ladies are often very attractive; they've got an eye for colour, an eye for style and she will be pretty knowledgeable about measurements and so on.

JOAN

Yes, well, apparently she makes quite
a lot of outfits for Griff which
Sylvia's very jealous about, although she says
Belinda claims she hasn't made them
– but Sylvia sees Griff come
padding out of Belinda's on a
Sunday morning having stayed over
and he's wearing some trendy denim
jacket with a flamingo-pink lining
and some little leather shorts ... so
it sounds like Belinda's spoiling
him rotten and Sylvia just can't
keep up.

JERICHA

Yes. Look I'd say, Griff, if you're
reading this, I'd think about
packing up a little bag with all
your needfuls, perhaps your dog
bowl and any medication that you're
on, and perhaps move in with Belinda
and see how that goes.

JOAN

Sylvia says Griff has Viagra in his feed now,
because he's reached the stage
where he needs it. But he possibly
only needs it around Sylvia – whereas
Belinda prancing about in bra and
pants may be an altogether much
more exciting package for him?

JERICHA

There's no competition really, is there, Joan? And to Sylvia asking, 'Should I marry my dog' my answer would be: well, you'd have to ask the dog – does he want to marry you?! And I suspect, whatever language you might address him in, the answer would be a very firm NO.

JOAN

Well, in the video footage she sent in she claimed he was actually proposing to her – but you can see there, she's manipulating his jaw and making him say it. She's been forcing him to learn languages via this Duolingo app – everything from Pakistani to Persian, I mean for goodness sake!

JERICHA

Poor Griff! She's clearly forcing him into all sorts of things he's not into. And that's tragic for him. So sending love to you, Griff, if you're reading this.

JOAN

Yes, and I think Sylvia should really give up on this one and just let him go to Belinda. The heart wants what it wants ...

WHEN TO TAKE YOUR OWN LIFE

In Sylvia Bomberoon's case, her dog was clearly ready to settle down with Belinda, the much prettier, still fertile, lingerie-clad dressmaker. No surprises there. Belinda sent us some wonderful photos of her wedding to Griff and their honeymoon, skydiving in the Maldives, and we understand that on seeing these, Sylvia then went on to take her own life. This wasn't necessarily a bad thing and for many of you, you may also want to start thinking of some alternatives as your hormones now begin to head rapidly downhill.

You might consider one of the wonderful early menopause packages being offered by Dignitas, where one can take in some lovely sights whistling through the Alps by train, enjoy the all-you-can-eat fondue buffets and the slutty boozy bashes, before recording something light and frothy for your nearest and dearest on your iPhone and sitting down to face the final curtain.

But if taking your own life's not 'your thing', a fab option is simply booking into a care home now, as you're likely to secure a decent room with a sea view and will enjoy being the prettiest one there, amidst all the open-mouthed oldies, dribbling from every orifice.

'BUT WHAT IF WE'RE STILL HAPPILY MARRIED?'

You're living a lie. There are ladies who guys have tried and tried to divorce, but she simply won't go, and short of killing her, he is forced to pretend all is well. She drowns every meal in dollops of cream and butter claiming she just wants to 'spoil him' when in fact she's deliberately boosting his galloping obesity and underlying heart condition, thus rendering him wheelchair bound and no longer able to go out poking his pipe into rampant local widows. Maybe you even believe you and your ageing blue-lipped groom have a nice little routine with your coffee 'n' crossword morning, followed by civilised trips to National Trust properties come the afternoon, where you can fart your way around the gift shops and bulk up on flapjacks and pricey teas. But just when you hoped to be going on a boozy cruise, with your Judith Chalmers frosted lips, backless loafers and big white trousers, an elderly parent falls ill (and it's usually yours) and you're forced to let her move in, spelling actual disaster for any marriage.

Incredibly, some ladies have their mother on tap from the get-go, ensconced in the bedroom next to the master suite, ready to offer sex tips, spy on hubby or take her side in an argument. But sometimes this can seriously backfire ...

JOAN

'Dear Joan and Jericha, my mother
has been living with my husband and
myself since we married, as she
has health issues.
At first he said he didn't like
it, as he felt he couldn't be as
loud as he wanted during sex, but
recently he's been spending a lot
of time with her, rinsing out her

commode and staying up late. Last night I heard him grunting in her room and she was yelping, "I'm coming! I'm coming, Greg!" She's ninety-one and I'm really worried about her.' And that's from Dorothy Illeandy, in Budleigh.

JERICHA

Ah, Budleigh. Super area down by the sea there.

JOAN

Lovely teashops with very moist fruitcakes.

JERICHA

And the wonderful authoress Hilary Mantel of course lives down that way, I believe?

JOAN

Yes, you can hear the wind in her words, can't you? The salty spray splattering across Hilary's pages.

JERICHA

What a clever lady …

JOAN

Big-brained lady, she did that lovely one about the wolf, didn't she? *Wolf in the Hall*?

JERICHA

Yes. *Wolves of Willoughby Hall*, was it?

JOAN

I believe so ... nice little earner ... But getting back to Dorothy Illeandy, it's actually rather lovely that hubby's rinsing out her old mum Pat's commode.

JERICHA

Yes, so he might have thought, God I've got this ghastly old mother-in-law moving in, I've had enough already of the whinging and nagging of this ghastly witch of a wife Dorothy ...

JOAN

Yes, Dorothy is quite a harridan to look at. And then Mum is there, ninety-one, yes, essentially a skeleton, looking very close to death.

JERICHA

But with that super, slim look, which means you can wear absolutely anything, Joan.

JOAN

And she is! She's just in that stained nighty, no pants to speak of, and the eyes: just scooped-out hollows.

JERICHA

Black holes in the face, Joan, almost like a snowman with coals for eyes.

JOAN

Big old carrotty nose and literally almost twigs for hands, with that little wonky smile on her face.

JERICHA

That could well be a stroke, Joan … but look, I imagine this chap, what's his name?

JOAN

Greg, Greg Illeandy.

JERICHA

Greg Illeandy has thought, Well, at least Pat's not a big old fatty like Dorothy, and he's reached into his heart and thought, What can I do? I know, I'll go and rinse out her commode …

JOAN

And Dorothy says Greg has now taken to using the commode himself.

JERICHA

OK …

JOAN

So, he goes in there with Pat, plops himself down and passes his own brown sausages – and really makes a day of it.

JERICHA

Well, it's a day out isn't it, Joan?

JOAN

Or a day in …

JERICHA

It's like a throwback to nursery where you popped yourself on a potty and did your business and you could take as long as you liked, Joan.

JOAN

And what do you think was going on in there, with Greg's grunts and old Pat yelping, 'I'm coming! I'm coming, Greg!'

JERICHA

Well, there are any number of explanations, Joan. The grunting might in fact have been her straining on the potty, or him trying to get off the potty.

JOAN

Dorothy said it was a male grunting, a pumping 'n' grunting.

JERICHA

All right, a pump and a grunt. Well, what occurs to me is if you've sat on a commode for too long, Joan, you can get substantial vacuum suction, so if you stand up it gets stuck to your bottom and you end up carrying it round all day.

JOAN

Also, he's going on top of Pat's stools.

JERICHA

Pat's big pile of old grey stools, so it's going to be pretty full with their joint Jenga stool tower and it won't take much to create a vacuum.

JOAN

So, Greg's tried to stand up, the commode's stuck to his botty, he's pumping and grunting trying to wrench it off …

JERICHA

He's panicking that when it does come off, those stools will go flying across the room and hit poor Pat in the face.

JOAN

But she's sat there, rather sweetly obviously wanting to help Greg, so she's shouting, 'I'm coming, I'm coming!'

JERICHA

Exactly, Joan.

JOAN

Now, in her longer letter, Dorothy says her mother Pat, then shouted, 'Fuck me! I want your big fat cock! Greg! Give me your big fat cock!'

JERICHA

OK, well look, it could be a fitful dream, Joan. The elderly do sleep a lot …

JOAN

Or could it be that Greg's taken a chicken in there for some company?

JERICHA

The elderly do keep odd pets down by the seaside. So it could be that the cock wakes Pat up every morning and she simply wants to have a little play with it.

JOAN

Dorothy goes on to say that Mum then shouted, 'I want your hard cock in my mouth.'

JERICHA

Well, yes she's hungry, Joan ... and this could be quite a fit, hardy cockerel dwelling by the sea.

JOAN

Dorothy says Pat then screamed, 'I want your cum in my mouth, Greg!'

JERICHA

OK, gosh well, what a mystery, Joan! I mean, I suppose it's possible that this Greg fellow, he's on the commode, he's got himself a little erection as men often do when they're defecating, and he's accidentally plopped out a white, semeny dribble that's landed in the old woman's porridge bowl and she's thought, you know what? I rather like the look of that creamy topping.

Perhaps dear old Pat Illeandy really was enjoying her son-in-law's firm penis in her ancient mouth. We'll never know. But the truth is many exhausted single ladies are not after a carnal companion at all, but simply some understated and pleasant platonic company! And just as there are dogs to guide the blind and cats to speak to the deaf, so there are birds to tend to the lost and the lonely.

It's MISTER COCKAPY!

For older single ladies of a nervous disposition, MISTER COCKAPY is a therapy cockatiel guaranteed to cheer you up, keep you company and perform small household chores. MISTER COCKAPY comes with his own silk waistcoat, tiny round glasses, mini cigarette and real mahogany snooker cue. And with a change of clothes for special occasions and casual nightwear to boot, he's quite the catch!

This little fella can clean up the kitchen table and down the back of the sofa, will make basic conversation, enjoy boxsets with you and loves to peck off unsightly skin tags and stubborn back hair. He can also check inside your mouth for gum disease and remove rotting food from between your teeth after a hefty takeaway.

It's more fun than flossing, ladies! So get your MISTER COCKAPY today!

Chapter 8

WHY YOU LOOK LIKE A TOMATO

All Change For The Menopause Express

For many women, as they start to head towards the end of life in their late forties and early fifties, everything begins to widthen and collapse. Facial, front botty and anal bearding accelerates and the breasts become hairy and depressed. 'The Change' is used by lots of ladies as an excuse to become tubby and rude, often becoming closer in appearance to an elderly, rusty-hued primate and somehow thinking it's acceptable to lash out, only stopping short of throwing her faeces about at family gatherings.

Around this time, however, hubby will be looking sexier than ever. Also having filled out from plenty of fatty breakfasts and all-day boozing, come summertime he'll love to don his budgie smugglers and parade his big mahogany belly and tubbied pubic pouch to young female guests or camel-toed divorcees alike, as he prances about with his barbecue tongs at your regular Sunday gatherings. With his groin bulging through his apron with boobs on, he'll be trying it on with every one of the opposite sex, and then offer you facelift vouchers later if you dare to complain. The fact is, your blummin' lucky this fella's stuck around at all.

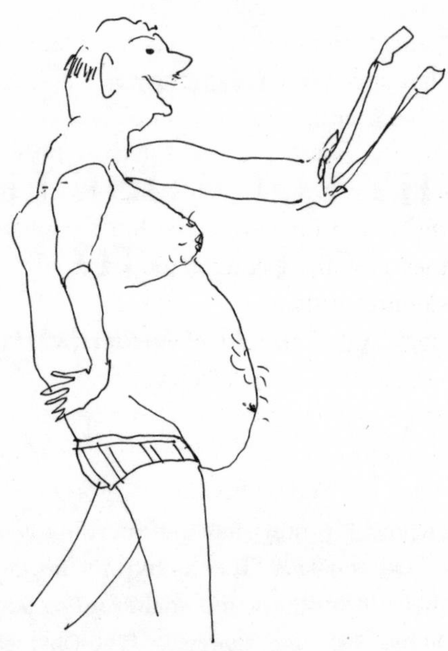

And as if these poor guys don't already have enough to deal with, they are then expected to share their bed with this tomato-faced wife in her sweaty old nighty, poking and prodding him all night because he's snoring! Ladies, please! The poor chap is thankfully getting a fab night's shut-eye after his boozy barby, which should be reward in itself! Is it his fault if he's beached on his back as the air buffets about his fat, bogie-filled nose, so he's honking from both ends having gorged on too many sausages?

THE LAST PENIS

For most of you, the challenges of 'The Change' and the decline of your marriage will coincide with your children entering the maelstrom of their teenage years, as many of you simply left pregnancy too late! Perhaps you were trying to 'have a career' or were hanging on for 'Mr Right', but in the end, you hopped on the last gasp penis that would take you. Meaning not only were you the most haggard mother at the school gates, with badgery hair and jowls that frightened all the little ones, you were consistently shunned by the hot Lycra mums having filthy flings with the teachers, excluded from all their 'wine o'clock' girly shindigs and Botox parties – and now everyone thinks you're an embarrassing grandmother creepily spending too much time 'hanging' with some blossoming teens.

Fortunately for the majority of us, our teenagers will be safely incarcerated in boarding school, meaning they will be mostly watched over by depressed teachers and the odd rum monk. So any perceived wrongdoings from our bald brethren swelling beneath their brown dresses, will, at least, create a diversion from the type of belligerent or illegal teen behaviour for which you might ordinarily be held accountable. It gives you a very valid excuse, in fact, should young Atticus or Roberta become a drug dealer and a prostitute later in life. At least you won't get the blame – the monk will take the rap.

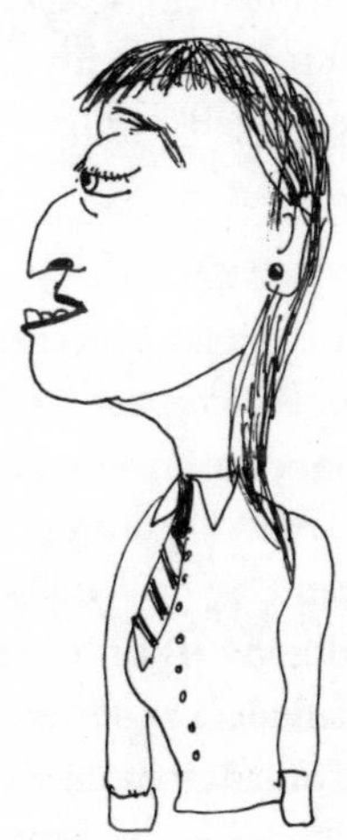

STINKY OAFS

But there are always the holidays when we do have to tolerate these stinky oafs lounging about the place. And 'stinky' goes for both sexes here, at this age. As always, an oniony boy masturbating until his sheets snap is still more tolerable than a fishy teenage girl with all-day morning breath and a jutting lower lip. The hooded eyes and hunched huffing of a lolling lass in the grip of puberty can be hugely taxing for mad menopausal mums, and must be shut down by either locking this moody miss in her bedroom (or cellar), or sedating her entirely during her period.

If, however, your daughter's friends are particularly attractive, be wary, ladies. Tubby Hubby may well be getting his baldy head turned by young Priscilla's hot chums, with their urging breast buds and the heady whiffs of their fluffy golden vulvas wafting up his eager nostrils. If he's forever clasping at an erection whenever her white-pantied girlfriends come round for pillow fights and slumber parties, don't try and fight it. If anything, allow him to get whipped into a purple-faced frenzy as he forces a bulging eye through their bedroom door and bashes his groin repeatedly against the door-knob. Just make sure you're nearby with a tube of KY ready to hop aboard his fattened stalk and relieve him of his bursting teste juice. It may just be your last chance.

JOAN

'Dear Joan and Jericha, I recently discovered
images of another woman's vagina on my
husband's phone and realised it belonged to
his boss's wife. When I confronted him he said
it was for a painting he was planning to do,
although he doesn't paint. Eventually things
came to a head and he admitted
they're having an affair, but he says it's for me

... if he keeps her happy, the boss is happy and so my husband's job is safe – and we can continue our lavish lifestyle.' And that's from Julie Wollygug, aged forty-nine, from Rye.

JERICHA

Oh, Joan, these ladies. You could absolutely bash them over the head with a saucepan, couldn't you? I mean, it's as plain as the nose on your face that poor Ryan Wollygug, down in Rye, is making the best of a tricky situation – and fulfilling his creative side at the same time, by the sound of it. He's seen the beauty of a young lady's part and understood that since time immemorial, artists have painted lovely females and all their bits and bobs for men to drool over and quite rightly so!

JOAN

Indeed. And in terms of this very dowdy lady Julie Wollygug, writing in and griping whilst clearly rather enjoying this high life ...

JERICHA

Yes, is that a Gucci bag she's got over her shoulder there?

JOAN

Oh, I mean she's top to toe in labels – I don't really know why she's complaining. This guy is an artist and he's having this very time-consuming, physically exhausting affair with the boss's wife, albeit an extremely attractive woman – a lot more attractive than Julie Wollygug despite all the fancy clothes, because as we know you can't make a silk purse out of a sow's ear.

JERICHA

And the silk purse you're alluding to, I imagine, Joan, is this younger lady's rather wonderful vulva that Ryan Wollygug is dutifully penetrating.

JOAN

Yes, I mean it's positively glistening there in the picture, isn't it?

JERICHA

Yes, almost like a Fabergé egg, Joan, in its beauty and precision. I'm even wondering, Joan, whether Mahmoud hasn't had some hand in all this?

JOAN

Very possibly. I know that Julie Wollygug says in her longer letter that she's not happy with her downstairs front. She's had a lot of other procedures but she's not managed to get around to improving that area.

JERICHA

No, and looking at the picture she's enclosed of her rather funny little baggy offering, there's no comparison, Joan. You're looking at a Fabergé egg and what – a messy omelette in comparison?

JOAN

A messy omelette that the dog's had a go at and brought back up.

JERICHA

Yet Ryan Wollygug hasn't left Julie and her eggy downstairs mess, he's selflessly gone about painting and pumping Renata's Fabergé vulva, spinning all these plates, poor guy, keeping her happy so the boss is happy, so that Julie Wollygug can continue her life in head-to-toe designer.

JOAN

He's a saint is Ryan Wollygug.

JERICHA

And I'd be very interested to see the finished painting, Joan.

JOAN

Yes, well we're both huge love art lovers.

JERICHA

We're buffs, Joan.

JOAN

Now, of course Mahmoud entered portrait artist of the year, didn't he? Having done those wonderful portraits of both of us ...

JERICHA

Yes. I rather felt like Kate Winslet in *Titanic* posing for him.

JOAN

You opted to go fully naked, didn't you?

JERICHA

Well, I kept my necklace on! But it just felt right, Joan. My choice.

NO-PONG-PUSS PANTS!

These big pretty panties have a heavily perfumed gusset, soaking up all those nasty lady pongs throughout the day, whilst the mini detergeridildo puffs pure bleach up into the uterus, keeping you industrial clean.

'Can I ask a gentleman to tease down my No-Pong-Puss Pants as part of foreplay?'

Ladies, please! Men don't have time for foreplay and much as we have made every attempt to pretty up the No-Pongs, with lacy edging or the naughty thong version, it's altogether more pleasant for the guy if you've removed your No-Pongs in the bathroom before intercourse, had a good scrub down with some anti-bacterial wipes and given yourself a quick once-over with a tooth or toilet brush.

You can then confidently engage in copulation, knowing if you smell of anything 'down there', it's bleach! Yes, there will be a complete drying out and shrivelling, but that means a tighter, smaller vagina for him. It also means a complete lack of lubrication. Some fellas are all over this, loving the lack of 'give' but if that doesn't float his willy boat, for an extra £250 we'll throw in the 'SO-Silky-M'Puss' purse spray. Just one sexy squirt and you've created a wonderful slick for your gung-ho guy to really pump himself into!

OLD PRAWNS TRAPPED IN A RADIATOR

One of the issues illustrated in the letter above (apart from Ryan Wollygug's saintly behaviour) is the disparity between Julie Wollygug's and Renata's vulvas. Not just in looks, but very probably in terms of scent. The hard facts are: left to their own devices, most ladies' genitals will end up ponging like old prawns trapped in a radiator.

Middle-aged lasses really do need to sit up and smell the downstairs coffee on this one – we've seen far too many a marriage break down because of it. Both your son and husband will be attuned to fresh floral pudendas, so the old beef you're packing will have them heading out the door and straight to the pub. And this type of difficult lady-whiff can also unwittingly keep extended family and friends away. Which is why Mahmoud designed **No-Pong-Puss Pants**!

WHY YOUR SON HATES YOU

But it's not just Dad who's struggling with Mum around this time. Sons especially find Mum intensely irritating and unsightly, and it could be wise for her to simply move out of the family home (just as menstruating ladies in some countries are, quite rightly, put into separate huts during their time of bleeding).

JOAN

'Dear Joan and Jericha, I have very big calves and wonder if there's anything I can do about it? My son says it puts him off his dinner, which I don't understand, as I keep them under the table and mostly wear trousers.'

Maud Trussell, Lytham St Annes.

JERICHA

Well, I know two people from Lytham St Annes, both slender-calved ladies, so it's certainly not genetic to the area.

JOAN

Are there particular hotspots around the UK where you might find pockets of bigger-calved ladies?

JERICHA

Yes, absolutely, there's certainly a concentration of these bulky-calved lasses in places like Newcastle and East Anglia where cousins often wed, so she likely originates from one of those places.

JOAN

Looking at this photo here, her calves really are so wide it's almost as if she has a buttock at the bottom of each leg.

JERICHA

Yes, those are very unsightly, but also ringing some alarm bells for me, Joan, because they may well be growths of some kind.

JOAN

Like tumours?

JERICHA

Big bulgy tumours, yes.

JOAN

But both exactly the same size and shape?

JERICHA

Well, yes, you do sometimes get these 'twin tumours', Joan, that sort of grow in cahoots and communicate with each other. What sort of age is this lady, would you say?

JOAN

She says forty-four.

JERICHA

She hasn't aged well, I'd put at least two decades on that, but yes, almost certainly that's what these growths will be.

JOAN

They actually look like two giant hams.

JERICHA

Well, I suppose they could be.

JOAN

As if she's just stuffed two giant hams into her tum and they've shot down her legs?

JERICHA

Well, in all honesty, it may be that they've not digested properly – very possible if she's not particularly active, which looks likely given that mottled corned-beefy skin. I feel sorry for this poor teenage son.

JOAN

Roy Trussell?

JERICHA

Yes, poor Roy there, with Mum slopping about in her shorty nighty.

JOAN
And that's very short, isn't it?
Only just skimming her vagina,
everything's tumbling out ...

JERICHA
Which can be very nice for some
sons, but not in the case of this
rather wretched, drum-legged old
trollopy mum.

JOAN
And you can see in the photo, young
Roy Trussell is looking directly at
Mum's tumbling bacon.

JERICHA
Yes, poor lad, he's getting a flash
of something he'd hoped probably
never to see in his lifetime.

JOAN
But he's still hiding the
beginnings of an erection.

JERICHA
Well look, that just shows the
sheer force of the male drive.
I'm pleased for him and if he's
getting engorged over Mum's ghastly meat
mess, imagine
what he'll do let loose amongst
some young pretty vaginas.

BOOB CHEESE

Another issue for declining lasses around this age can be a surfeit of what's medically termed 'Boob Cheese' or 'Booby Butter'. This banana-coloured gunk collects inside a lady's bra as she goes about her day, profusely sweating into her bra cups, so by bedtime there's enough fromage gathered to make a sandwich! Not only is this ghastly if poor old hubby spots your yellowed cups, but, boy, does it whiff!

You can always encourage a family pet, such as a large Labrador or a willing whippet, to snuffle about your discarded bra and hoover up your boob cheese (the smaller dogs can't manage it), but chances are he'll bring it all back up on the hall carpet or have a bad reaction and pass away, noisily, during one of hubby's all important business dinners.

As always, Mahmoud and his wiry associate Dr Graham Nupp are at the forefront in offering support to menopausal women in areas such as this. The BoobCheese Bra was developed primarily by Dr Nupp, after years of his mother Gwynne, with whom he lodged, being a martyr to the condition, often creating up to six pounds of cheese a day. Sadly, she's since passed away.

BOOBCHEESE BRA

The **BoobCheese Bra**, with its extra wide detachable tubing around the cup, sucks all your breast cheese away so that you can enjoy your day, bending, reaching and stretching without any unsightly cheese leaks. Simply pipe it out later into the pretty cheese pouch and no one need ever know what your boobs were up to!

Most ladies think they must toss this shameful cheesy pouch straight in the bin, but just as breast milk is yummy and nutritious, so this sour and sweaty boob gunk can be recycled to make a bold cheese souffle or a thick sauce, with the same strong scrotal tang guys love when eating goat's cheese.

Also available, the '**GrannyCheese Bra**' for elderly ladies with mouldy, Stilton-like lumps collecting under their shrivelled frontal chest flaps.

Disclaimer: Do not use collected granny boob cheese in any recipe for humans or animals as it may cause convulsions.

These freshening aids can help to some degree but the fact is if hubby hasn't already given you the old heave-ho, he's certainly gearing up to it, if not googling ways to have you quietly done away with. Some of you may still believe you can be the one to leave him and start afresh, but in truth we all know you'll live out your last days solo, beadling about some Suffolkian village buying endless jugs and poking your veiny hooter into everyone's business in an attempt to destroy their marriages too.

Others may take a jolly deep breath and throw themselves into the competitive arena of the LOLs (late onset lesbians), hefting their danglies about, hoping a large tattoo or a few piercings might seal the deal, or setting themself up as a spiritual healer in the hope of some stolen gropes. That said, it seems ladies in church choirs do fare rather well and lesbians are surprisingly open to the plain and the hefty.

PANTLESS FELLAS

There is another, smaller portion of late life ladies who instead of retreating, start loudly bleating on about how they need more pampering and 'me time', often seeking out dubious guru types for guidance, some of whom claim to be yogis (having done a weekend course in Ibiza). Often hessian-trousered, pantless fellas, they can allegedly manifest oils from their palms, don't wear deodorant and absent-mindedly nudge their clearly outlined penis against ladies faces when performing 'healing' massage. Truth be told, many a menopausal Mrs is actually going to these guys solely for this purpose, turning their dry, desperate mouths towards his wandering willy in the hope of a wet, clothy nibble, before tea.

But such is the act of the desperate and the deluded. In order to be part of the successful few who do manage to hang on to Hubby, you need to really start thinking outside the box when it comes to his mid-life sexual needs.

JOAN

'Dear Joan and Jericha, my wife says she has the menopause and that intercourse is painful. It's certainly very dry and baggy as far as I'm concerned, and although I can give myself a nice big erection from thumbing through the *Radio Times*, I lose it as soon as I look at my wife.

So I recently suggested I urinate in her mouth but she burst into tears and said she wanted a divorce – and then said she was going to wee on me, see how I liked it, but then she couldn't go.

What should I do?'

Niall Combuss, Ealing

JERICHA

Hello, Niall! What a great guy to suggest water sports with this woman who makes his penis flop.

JOAN

Yes, she's very silly, this Carol Combuss, to say she wants a divorce when she's clearly hanging on by a thread.

JERICHA

And very nasty. Because a guy offering to urinate into a lady's mouth is actually incredibly romantic.

JOAN
And he's obviously happy to be
urinated on as well.

JERICHA
But she couldn't manage it, oh
dear.

JOAN
Yes, she looks like a very
dehydrated sort of lass to me, the
type that dribbles that thick gravy-type urine.

JERICHA
Yes, very dense, Joan, and brown –
almost solid.

JOAN
With that pungent soupy whiff ... No,
guys are after that gorgeous golden
straw-coloured urine, aren't they?

JERICHA
Indeed, the Britt Ekland in her
youth kind of urine.

JOAN
Absolutely. Now Niall says in his
longer letter he wants to urinate
from really quite a height.

JERICHA
OK, sure, well let's start with
practical considerations – how
high, what sort of furniture does

he have to climb on? I've got a
great gentleman friend who has
actually had a platform built at
the top of his grand central
staircase with a hole in it.

JOAN

How gorgeous … sort of sounds like
Grand Designs.

JERICHA

Yes, well it is actually Kevin
McCloud …

JOAN

Wonderful presenter.

JERICHA

… who as you are aware, Joan, I know
socially – Cardinal had a fling
with his niece. Now I'm not
suggesting for a minute
that Kevin is into
water sports of a sexual nature;
let's not start flying around with
all these speculations! It's up to
Kevin and his multiple partners
what he does and doesn't get up to –
there's really nothing to dwell on
here or fantasise about in that
way …

JOAN

No, but these kind of special stair
platforms can have this super hole

for the man to put his penis
through, can't they? So he can then
pee down and try and aim it into
the lady's mouth.

JERICHA
Indeed.

JOAN
Niall also says he'd love to taste the wee of a
lady who's just been jogging.

JERICHA
But not a lady with a UTI, I presume?

JOAN
No, that would be very tangy! He's sixty and
what's nice is he likes to
involve ladies of his own age, but
his real desire is to wee up a
lady's nose – and he's finding it
hard to get someone to agree.

JERICHA
OK, but he's already looking outside the
marriage which is good. I mean, it might be
worth this Niall Combuss perhaps going a bit
older still, maybe he could log on to a
specialist website?

JOAN
Yes, or just have a wander into an old people's
home? I'm sure there'd be plenty of willing
recipients in there happy to have a penis
nudged up their nose in exchange for a nice
box of Cadbury's Heroes.

Yet another example of a fun hubby, in this case Niall, trying to spice things up but dreary old Carol simply won't play ball. And, yes, it's true that ladies can be prone to thick brown urine and continual cystitis around this time and will often find that their womb has actually fallen out into their pants. So now's the time to get practical. If everything has collapsed around the front, you should frankly be making more effort to spruce things up 'out back', so that if hubby should become interested after a few bottles of wine, then he's able to park his pork where the sun don't shine.

Here again our dear friends Mahmoud and the fleet-of-foot Dr Nupp come hoving into view with another of their wonderful devices.* This one's for the ladies whose back botty, 'Botty Two', has begun to shrivel and seal over, like a lonely mollusc coming to the end of its natural life.

* All of which are trialled on willing rodents and grateful sausage dogs, that would otherwise be drowned in the canal after Christmas.

THE STRETCHY

Inspired by the metal eye clamp used in the film *A Clockwork Orange*, '**THE STRETCHY**' is Mahmoud's favoured method for anal stretching. The stretchy is secured around the anus using its pretty sani-belt and braces (which come in Wall Street Red), and can be worn under pyjamas or simply on a naked body (which is a huge turn on for those who enjoy clowns or S&M).

Simply dollop a blob of Vaseline deep into the anus using the handle of a wooden spoon and ask a partner or family member to secure the metal clamp in place, spreading the anus to almost breaking point. Then go to sleep. By morning the anus will have lost 50 per cent of its elasticity and capacity to grip, leaving you with a much baggier anal sleeve and affording your hubby the ability to now enjoy a wide range of activities which were previously unmanageable.

THE STRETCHY itself comes in a pretty rose gold or simple sterling silver, in stark contrast to the bright red braces, and every Stretchy is personally engraved with Mahmoud's distinctive signature, which he crafts using his wonderful but surprisingly sharp-ended nose.

Aside from all the positives, it can come with the small side effect of unwanted stools escaping throughout the day, which is why Dr Nupp includes a multi-pack of his own range of scented hammock pants, which will catch and perfume even the heftiest lady stools, allowing you to go about your day as normal. The scented hammock pants come in **Saucy Sir, Hot 'n' Heavy, Simply Beige and Sulky Slut**.

THE BOTTY BOMB

Most guys have haemorrhoids or 'piles' (see also 'botty grapes', 'bum raisins', 'blood nuts') which don't tend to bother them, and ladies should still be happy to digitally or orally pleasure their guy's sore or exploded anus whenever he needs.

But when a lady, particularly around this menopausal age, has this condition, it's repulsive and no gentleman should ever have to know 'what lies beneath'. Women with bad botty grapes do tend to bring it on themselves. They are often pear-shaped, resentful types, who mindlessly snack on doughy treats and grunt on the toilet for hours (often in the comfort of a neighbour's more attractive bathroom) only to pass grey, stale-smelling pellets, and stinking out their friend's home whilst her family tries to eat dinner. Botty bombs (little carbon balls which one inserts last thing at night and then lights with a long party match) will remove piles in a small, controlled explosion and are available in most pharmacies and hardware stores (and some of the classier supermarkets like Waitrose or M&S). They come in a pack of five with a miniature shovel, along with the special Naughty-Night-Blaster Pants to catch any overnight leakage. Do be sure to insert them on a Saturday evening and let them go to work throughout the night. By morning your Blaster Pants will be full of your exploded piles and then you're good to go!

And talking of soiled undies, it is with great regret that we must inform you, dear readers, that we have reached our final chapter … where we must join those ageing, crumbly ladyfolk, shuffling and stumbling into their twilight years, the Randy Reaper forever tugging at their desiccated nethers …

Chapter 9

WHY HE WISHES YOU WERE DEAD

Sex Surges And Trapped Wind In The Elderly Lady

One of life's great ironies is that once the menopause is done and dusted, and all the whingeing and whining has been ignored into silence, a lady's sexual urges often begin once more to soar. Meaning many an elderly gent has been awoken on Christmas morn by his previously sexually defunct wife clambering aboard his love boat bod and grinding her pelvis energetically atop his face.

For some men, this is a wonderful time of renewal and rediscovery. But for most, it is an appalling shock, often resulting in a series of cluster heart attacks or a full-blown escalation of any lurking cancers. Of course, some old hubbies are delighted that their crumbling old member is being noticed after decades of shunning, but mostly they wish the woman smothering his toothless face was not his wife with her ancient pudenda, grunting and parping away as she frenziedly bounces her osteoporotic-riddled hips astride his bristly chin, but rather a lithe and agile young hooker.

MY HUSBAND WANTS AN AFFAIR

JOAN

'Dear Joan and Jericha, my husband
is seventy-nine and recently told me he's
been thinking about having an
affair because he's so bored and
because I keep breaking loud,
stinky wind during intercourse.
What should I be doing to keep him
from leaving me?'
Sue Bollins, seventy-three, from Chichester

JERICHA

Well, stop farting for a start
please, Sue!

JOAN

Yes, unfortunately Sue says in her longer letter that she has a spastic colon, so she can't help it.

JERICHA

Well, she can help it, actually. But if she insists on doing it, she'll need to combine some very loud music during intercourse with a hefty perfume to try and distract poor Don Bollins from all these loud and stinky botty shrieks.

JOAN

She says she'd love to try and talk dirty to Don, but she doesn't know what to say. Her friend suggested that you can give a commentary of what you're doing?

JERICHA

Not advisable in her case, Joan, because that will be, 'I'm doing a big stinky fart on your penis, Don.' No, look, I'd have to say, this Sue Bollins is living in cloud cuckoo land anyway because Don Bollins will already have had numerous affairs, and this is just his way of getting it out on the table. So it's actually very kind of him.

JOAN

And he's a great-looking guy, isn't he? With that salt 'n' pepper bowl cut and that almost lilac skin that eczema sufferers have.

JERICHA

Gorgeous, yes, the pinky-grey hue, with lots of flakes hanging off there, particularly around Don's very long nose. And the eczema exposes this very raw skin which is actually making Don look a lot younger.

JOAN

Yes, like a sort of boiled lizard in his late forties ... So if Sue is looking to fancy-up a sex session, how long should the session be?

JERICHA

Well, it could be anything from twenty seconds, Joan, up to a fortnight – with food being brought in!

JOAN

OK, so let's try and step into Sue and Don Bollins's boots for a moment. They've had a nice bottle of red and a big shepherd's pie, they've got themselves in the mood after some telly ... either a sexy romcom ...

JERICHA

Yes, or a gruelling ITV drama about
a missing woman.

JOAN

I suppose Don would be rather tired
if he'd had to sit through a romcom?

JERICHA

Exactly, he'll be much livelier
after a grisly murder, Joan, with
the dismembered body of a partially
clothed young woman being found in
a wood. And he won't, in all honesty, be
wanting to think about Mrs Bollins when he
starts pumping away at her.

JOAN

No.

JERICHA

He'll want to be fantasising about
women he's seen on TV that day:
Carol Vorderman, Fiona Bruce ...

JOAN

Yes, a lot of these guys love the
older ladies, don't they? Mary
Berry, Delia Smith, Esther Rantzen.
It's not always the Kardashians
with their bouncy boobs and big
booties.

JERICHA

No, because as you can see from Don
Bollins's photo, he has these very

small hands, sort of mini banana fingers – and they simply couldn't get a purchase on that size booty. So he'll more likely want to jolt his own penis about with his mini banana hands and have a good think about someone he's seen on a quiz show that afternoon.

JOAN

Rather than this awful lump of a wife on top, desperately trying to think of new positions?

JERICHA

Yes, I mean look, Sue could attempt a simple doggy position or a reverse cowgirl, but Don risks a very nasty blast in the face if he's not careful.

JOAN

She says she's always loved giving hand jobs, but now has very arthritic fingers.

JERICHA

Well, that's nonsense, Joan, she could always adapt one of these litter grabbers if necessary.

JOAN

Yes, she could stuff a rubber glove with cotton wool, attach it to the litter grabber and warm it on the radiator. That will likely pass as a real hand, as far as Don's concerned.

JERICHA
And if she can afford two of these grabbers, she could use the other one to be poking about Don's bottom, or at the very least be making him a snack for afterwards.

Happily, we heard later from Sue that Don had found the confidence to leave her for a young curvaceous lady who was delivering their meals on wheels. Don and Precious are now living in student accommodation with four other youngsters, and Don has recently joined a heavy metal band – and never been happier.

DRY AND CRUSTY

Whether she's making love or not, many an older lady will feel a bit crackly and dry in all areas, particularly her Botties One and Two. Here's a recipe that Jericha grew up with to assist in the moistening of these arid orifi.

MOTHER'S CREAMY NIGHT CRUMBLIES

My long departed mother, Fanny Domain,* was a tiny but fierce female boxer who only ever needed two hours' sleep, but religiously took her Creamy Night Crumblies to keep herself internally moisturised in case my father needed to let off steam during the night.

---

* See Appendix B.

He, in turn, was a whopping fellow, devoutly religious and hugely blessed below. Donald, as he was known, only enjoyed two lovemaking positions: one was with my mother still in her big round gloves, on her back, her face covered with a pillow right up until his climax, when he would lift it off her and then slam it back down again. The other position he favoured was the wheelbarrow (though due to their height discrepancy it became the flying wheelbarrow) and I could often hear my father whizzing Mum about the room as he gathered pace.

Even in her boxing dotage, she had the skin of an angel inside and out, thanks to her Creamy Night Crumblies. These are small balls of crunchy goodness that I would recommend to all ladies over thirty.

INGREDIENTS

You'll need:
A pound of shea butter
4 crushed mice spines
1 large tin of molasses
Half a mug of Cornish cream
1 bag of stale bashed biscuits

METHOD

Smash everything up with a fat wooden spoon, mould into large lozenges and deep fat fry.

These can be eaten through the mouth or inserted below (on the end of wooden spoon handle as part of elderly foreplay) as a nourishing pessary. They also work well for anal dryness, particularly if this randy miss is after some backstreet action.

UPSCALE YOUR SECRET WEAPONS

So what can these doddery ladies do to turn their old fellas on? Well let's remember, one of the main reasons any man marries a lady is simply because she has boobs.

Of course, all men would prefer the taut buds of a younger woman of, say, fourteen. But even as a very elderly lady, don't forget you still have the weapon of your boobs – if you know how to work them right!

JOAN
We actually get a lot of letters
from women in their eighties and nineties
wanting to have boob jobs, don't we,
Jericha? And relatives say no,
it's too late.

JERICHA
It's never too late for a boob job,
Joan.

JOAN
So should these very elderly ladies
go for the big hard bowling-ball
boob like Posh Spice? Or a more
sexy French boob with the
peaking up, puppy nose nipple?

JERICHA
I do think the peaking puppy nose
is very pretty and enyouthening.

JOAN
Even though the rest of the body
has collapsed?

JERICHA

Well, look, she can experiment.
There's this new service where you can
try on a prosthetic version of
your favourite style boobs and your
cosmetic surgeon will then pop on some
dirty R&B – and our elderly lady will then
strip for him, jiggling the
fake hooters to see if he gets a
bumpy frontage beneath his
operating gown.

JOAN

Then *boom*! You know you've found
the right boob! And how about nipples?

JERICHA

Older guys are often blind, so ideally
they need big, tough, braille-style nipples to
grip on to, to find their way around.

JOAN

And actually, more and more animal
nipples are becoming available now.

JERICHA

Yes, dog nipples are taking off – I know
Camilla Parker Bowles recently had a set
put on. She went with some sturdy
Labrador ones which Charles adores
and he's known to have a very doggy,
furry penis himself.

JOAN

Well, his trousers always look full! Now I know another issue we do find with the geriatric boob is these poor old ladies still need their mammograms, but a common problem is the breast being squashed flat and then never springing back. So what can one do about this?

JERICHA

Unfortunately very little, Joan, as the breast at this age is mostly made of air.

JOAN

Could hubby blow the boob back up through the nipple?

JERICHA

Well, most of these oldies won't have much puff, but he could use a bicycle or balloon pump – which would at least give our lady a two-hour window of a reinflated breast, for an evening at the theatre, or a ruby anniversary 'do'.

JOAN

My mother Joan Senior* has always had fab boobs that she loved to show off, but once she hit eighty the nipples sort of joined up.

---

* See Appendix B.

JERICHA

Yes, 'boob-fusing', Joan, very common at this age. The theory being that due to lack of action, the nipples turn towards each other and before you know it they've fused into a fleshy brown bar, much like a handle.

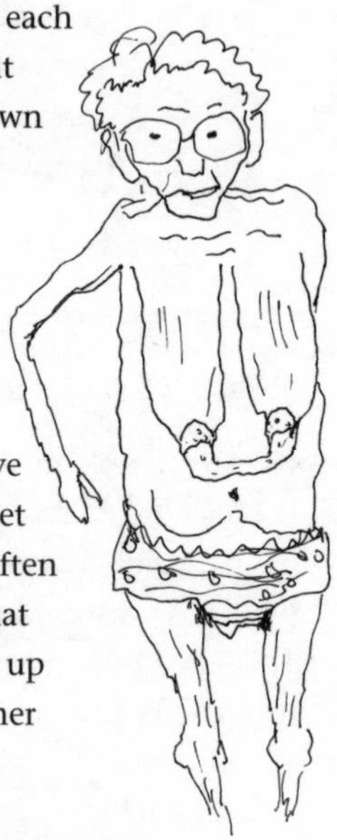

JOAN

So suddenly you've got a sort of breast handbag?

JERICHA

Yes, which some old boys love to suckle at, but it's hard to get any real purchase – and more often than not he's simply using that booby handle to hoist himself up and out of bed to go for another tinkle in his nightpot.

JOAN

Is there an operation should one wish to separate the nipples?

JERICHA

Yes, it's very simple, Joan, and can be a rather nice day out, actually. Old Evelyn can have her fleshy handle snipped and sealed, then she can coil up each nipple and pop them back into her bra cups, hop in the car, and her and hubby can shuffle about a National Trust property for the afternoon and shovel down a cream tea.

JOAN
And that's fun for hubby to then
have almost two curly straws to
suckle on when they get home?

JERICHA
Indeed, or in the castle car park!

JOAN
Bless!

HOCKEY STICK PENIS

Elderly hubbies really do deserve a big dollop of praise for sticking it out with these ghastly old biddies, but their true feelings are often liable to reveal themselves, as we've seen with a growing phenomenon in the long-wed gent called 'hockey stick penis'. This condition causes the penis to literally get bent out of shape, through its attempts to escape the old lady vagina.

Some randy ladies insist on forging ahead regardless, rabidly forcing hubby's right-angled member up themselves, in their frenzied lust for a wobbly elderly orgasm, but often end up bashing it right up through their bladders and into the caecum.

There have been cases of ladies developing 'hockey vagina' in later life, so hubby's reluctant trouser snake slots nicely into her angled chasm. But for everyone else, it can be trained with a special device – but only if the man is amenable of course!

JERICHA

Yes, this straightening device is actually based on a simple shoehorn. I'm familiar with this because very early in my sex life I met a man ... let's call him Peter Braithwaite.

JOAN

Was that his name?

JERCIHA

Yes. And Peter developed this hockey stick penis shortly after we started dating, despite only being in his thirties, but his was pointing downwards so when erect it would point out horizontally and then sharply down.

JOAN

Like a fleshy bathroom tap lurching towards you?

JERICHA

Exactly, Joan.

JOAN

Was that nice or frightening?

JERICHA

In the beginning it was quite nice, then I got a bit frightened and then repulsed. One day I said to Peter, 'Do you think we can do something about your "funny old penis",' as I called it, and he said he was willing to give it a go.

JOAN

So you got out your shoehorn?

JERICHA
Yes, I've always had a good imagination, Joan,
and I realised I could just flatten it and attach it
with some simple masking tape, and he wore
that at night, every night, for three years.

JOAN
OK and you're placing the penis on top
of the shoehorn?

JERICHA
Exactly, and then you manually
straighten the penis, force the end
up or down depending on the problem,
and tape it very firmly to the shoehorn.

JOAN
Poor you, though.

JERICHA
Yes … At least Ralph's member wasn't hockey
sticked?

JOAN
No, just too small, but it's a long time since
I've seen any action there – although he does
get erections whenever Gyulchay comes into
the room.

JERICHA
Does that bother you?

JOAN
I think it's just the smell of
dinner coming more than anything.

JERICHA

But, yes, getting back to Peter,
sadly it didn't work very well in
the end, because his penis became very
infected. He forgot to take the
tape off for a week by which time
the poor penis had blackened and
died.

JOAN

So that was the end of that?

JERICHA

Exactly. Obviously Peter's penis
ceased to function and anyway I was on the
lookout for a guy with something approaching
twenty-two inches, but he became
an avid gardener in the absence of
his own ability to pollinate, and
named a rose after himself: the Peter
Braithwaite Black-End, which is
yellow and purple with a black tip.

JOAN

Which is how it looked with the
septicaemia?

JERICHA

Indeed.

'WILL I BE FOREVER LONESOME?'

For the vast majority of you, though, hubby will have scarpered long since, meaning our lady is left to fend for herself in the downstairs department. But this need not spell disaster for the daring and the doughty!

DOGS AND DOWAGERS

What could be a nicer sight than an elderly lady perched in a wing-backed chair in her bungalow, looking out at the seaside? Her overly made-up eyelids daubed in the brightest powdery blue, her tiny old lips smeared huge and red like Ronald McDonald, a fox-head stole thrown about her shoulders and a dozen clumpy rings wedged on her still chubby fingers. As she wakes and dozes, emitting various grunts and puffs, a glass of port in one hand, a drooping cigarette in the other, we note that her skirts are bunched up and her drawers hooked about her withered ankles, as an eager little Pomeranian pants vigorously between her purpled thighs.

She knows hubby's run off with a much fruitier, plump-pussied young thing – but our clown-faced lady has not wasted any time in exploring the advantages of the favourite pet for the late-life lass: the lap dog. And like an Amsterdam prostitute, she sits proud as punch in full view of the day trippers and promenaders, allowing Little Mister Licky a short break from time to time, to observe his gathered audience and roll around on his fluffy back, legs agape to display his dangly doggy wares, before leaping back with his skilful, fiddlesome tongue to continue his afternoon duties with gusto. Bravo!

Some ladies, as we have seen, marry their dogs for the wonderful companionship and romantic outings,* whilst other simply randy dowagers want to pursue a purely physical relationship with one of our furry friends and are desperate for more information!

JOAN

So I understand now it's not just the licky wee lap dogs, but the larger hounds that are also in demand with their much bigger, stronger tongues, Jericha?

* Please see page 201.

JERICHA

Yes, as vaginas have increased in size, Joan, through ladies eating too many potatoes, these larger breeds such as the Great Danes and the St Bernards are very popular amongst the clitorally bulbous. And the bulldogs and Clumber spaniels, with their endless drool, are proving a big hit amongst big-vaginaed ladies suffering from baggy dryness.

JOAN

And given that these older ladies' lower regions are less palatable than their younger sisters', how do they attract these big dogs to get in amongst it?

JERICHA

Well, one used to just tip a can of Chum around the vulva, Joan, and hope for the best, but nowadays ladies sprinkle kibble there.

JOAN

That's the dry dog food?

JERICHA

Yes, so doggy's faeces are nice and firm, meaning he won't squirt butterscotch diarrhoea all over our lady's thighs, as she reaches her shuddering climax.

JOAN

But possibly a long dry stool?

JERICHA

Yes.

JOAN

OK. So she's popped the kibble around the vulva and up the vaginal canal?

JERICHA

Yes, and she can poke some up her anus too, Joan, and the dog will desperately lick around, trying to hook it out and get at it. They're very persistent a lot of these dogs.

JOAN

That's fab, and I believe there is a French pâté you can use too?

JERICHA

Yes, it's a lovely cunnilingual pâté from Bordeaux that you can squirt up yourself or smooth round your boobs or wherever you want the dog to really have a go at – so mixing kibble on the nipples with a squidge of pâté under the boob itself is a very nice combo indeed.

JOAN

But it's not just about going at the boobs and below, is it? A lot of these ladies do want a bit more seduction, even foreplay?

JERICHA

Yes, look, who doesn't love a sultry French kiss, Joan? And many of these dowagers don't have any teeth, so they can smear big clumps of the pâté along their gums and let the dog just get his tongue in there and really go to town, many of these dogs will 'kiss' for hours.

JOAN

Gorgeous! And then would you encourage, say, your St Bernard to pop his paws on your shoulders and maybe have a slow dance?

JERICHA

Yes, light some candles, Joan, pop on a bit of Elgar or some Elton John, to get him in the mood, and he won't be shy about showing you his big lipstick penis. And after your dance you can both enjoy some wonderful mutual pleasuring – and once satisfied, you can have your cigarette and he can have another bowl of Chum.

JOAN

Gorgeous. And as you say it's not a one-way street; all dogs love a blowie, don't they?

JERICHA

Of course. But don't expect him to be faithful! What many folk don't realise is that when these dogs are out on walks and they dash off into the bushes, ostensibly to fetch a ball, there's an awful lot going on that we don't normally see.

JOAN
Between the dogs?

JERICHA
Yes, male dogs will often lie end to end and give each other a little bit of oral round the back of Hampstead Heath. Head to tail. Not unlike human men in that area.

JOAN
Lovely. So what about travelling with a canine lover on cruises, or the Orient Express? How accepting are travel companies of these furry companions when you're booking?

JERICHA
Well, like the therapy dogs, Joan, if you say at the time of booking that it's a sex-dog, they're legally obliged to take both of you.

JOAN
OK, and these sex-dogs really do enjoy travel, stopping off for coffees, maybe meeting a wee stray to have a quick romp behind some bins, or a filthy holiday fling in a disused car park.

JERICHA
Exactly, but don't forget to take a ball or a squeaky toy to throw up and down the train corridor during the longer stretches of the journey, when he may get very bored and start humping other passengers, which can be hurtful.

OLDER RELIGIOUS LADIES

Some of our animal lovers have sent in pics of themselves with their sex pets (see picture section for details.) But what of our saintly sisters who have spent their life in service to their heavenly husband, but who, like all of us, have housed within their habits those bushy burgers brimming with violent sexual urges? They have had to quash these impulses through prayer and sufferance, but they too, are suddenly hostage to this rampant, late-life sex surge – and indeed it seems to afflict elderly nuns the most severely. As seen here in the case of Sister Mary Oderpin ...

JOAN

'Dear Joan and Jericha, I'm a lady of eighty-seven and have recently found myself rubbing my breasts, teasing my nipples and sometimes patting below until I climax at these girlie magazines I discovered in a nearby graveyard. I live in a nunnery with thirty other sisters and feel terribly ashamed, but also terribly attracted to most of them. I've lashed myself with wire wool dish scrubbers at night and have made myself drink my own and their urine from their night potties – and sometimes I've gorged on Mother Superior's stools. Sorry.' Mary Oderpin, Chichester

JERICHA

Oh goodness and that's Sister Mary, I imagine?

JOAN

Yes, apologies, very wobbly writing and the letter is stained yellow. Heartbreaking.

JERICHA

Probably dribbles of urine from her mouth, Joan. Dear oh dear.

JOAN

I know!

JERICHA

Well, look, Sister Mary's done the right thing in joining this Sacred Order to serve our Lord, but unfortunately, has not been able to fight this late-life sex surge … whereby, she's accidentally come across these pictures of big breasted

lovelies holding their glistening vulvas open
and she's then spent the whole evening
tweaking her nipples and tapping
her nethers, when she should have
been in holy contemplation.

JOAN

The problem is there are nasty local folk with
nothing better to do than push these dirty
magazines through nunnery letterboxes, or
plant them in the graveyard, with
collaged, pop-up scrapbooks of Page 3
boobs and splayed, bleached
botties, in order to try and tempt
these poor old horny nuns.

JERICHA

And most of Christ's brides are able to resist,
but not Sister Oderpin, perhaps because
she's been sitting on a lifetime's cauldron of
sex urges.

JOAN

Do you think she's right to be lashing herself
with the wire wool whips, drinking everybody's
urine and swallowing stools?

JERICHA

Well, on the one hand you've got to feel sorry
for her, Joan, scrabbling on her hands and
knees, her habit hitched up, poking about
under the beds, grasping at urine and faeces.
And on the other, you wonder, could she not
have sought out a randy monk to satisfy her
cravings? But perhaps that's still not what the

Lord ordered and maybe she wouldn't have been turned on by the junk in this monk's trunk – so ultimately, no, wire wool lashings never did anyone any harm.

JOAN

She says in her longer letter she longs to break free, but thinks if she entered normal society she'd be sexually assaulting women left, right and centre.

JERICHA

Yes, I think she would be a menace, Joan. Thank God there are no iPhones in the nunnery for her to google dirty films on.

JOAN

No, but she will have access to a rudimentary television set?

JERICHA

True, they tend to watch the Easter Service or Carols by Candlelight, from Westminster, don't they? But what worries me, Joan, is she may be sneaking down at midnight, having gobbled up some potty contents and lashed herself with the wire wool, her habit's bunched up and tucked into her big nun pants as she walks past the partly ajar TV room door and before you know it she's got the controls, she's scrolled through for one of these filthy sex channels and she's giving herself a right old seeing-to with the remote!

JOAN

Well, yes, she's actually sent a photo in, for whatever reason, of the remote control in question, and she's worn it down and tapered it into the shape of a rather battered phallus from all the overuse.

JERICHA

Well, look, there's not a lot we can suggest here. She could be more creative with the potty gobbling, you know, put everything into one giant pot, give herself a time limit, almost like a solo drinking game, Joan, where you have to take a sip every time you have a dirty thought ...

JOAN

Maybe she could start by simply confessing all to Mother Superior because she, at the very least, will be wondering where all her stools are going.

CARE HOME SLUT

We know that some of you will thankfully have had the foresight to book into the care home as early as fifty, much to the disappointment of any sons and daughters who were hoping to get their grabby hands on your wonga – but strap in, as you will now be joined by hordes of abandoned widows and bitter singletons dumped by their families, all vying to become the newest 'Care Home Slut'. As soon as these lady hordes arrive, they slather on the make-up and pump these half-dead guys full of Viagra, so they can ride their crumbling members from dusk until dawn.

With all the medication available to her, the Care Home Slut is like a kid in a candy shop, putting on impromptu performances and sexy striptease shows – and she will have no qualms about foisting herself on either sex, appearing suddenly in the accessible showers brandishing her pointy soap on a rope, or administering sexy bed baths and intimate creamings to men trying to quietly pass away.

Happily, this can also be a real renaissance for our old friends the Prowling Spinsters, who have suffered the life of the plain and dowdy, always scrabbling for scraps 'n' crumbs when it comes to the penis department. Suddenly she can heap on the lippie and garish wig and reinvent herself! She was a famous actress! A fashion designer! A promiscuous model! She blathers on to her captive audience, waddling about, mounting poles and jiggling her stringy boobs and ancient booty at the more senile residents whenever it takes her fancy, knowing she can play the 'disinhibition card' if there are any complaints from concerned relatives.

And it won't be difficult for her to find out which elderly gent has the most 'cash in the attic' and persuade him, using her gummy and very blowjobbable mouth, into a dramatic, death bed marriage! She can even enjoy a bit of open coffin straddling in the front room before they come to take him away, and then pop it on her Instagram. Happy days.

So there you have it, ladies. Everything you need to know from A to Z when it comes to guys! We do, of course, love to hear all your success stories apart from ones that are clearly made up (or where you sound rather braggy and obnoxious). And again we must reiterate, any soiled pants or bodily emissions (apart from perhaps the odd tub of sperm from someone very hunky!) are not welcome as they do tend to go mouldy in the post.

For those of you with any complaints, we are afraid we are not legally able to respond to you and it's very likely that your continued lack of success is due to incurable shortcomings on your part, so please, no threatening messages, we do have our contacts, but would rather not feel forced into using them, thank you very much.

We will be offering some online one-on-one, two-on-one and two-on-two Skype sessions for those of you particularly in need, and why not try our guided intercourse sessions for the unsightly and the elderly, or our slow masturbation for single hunky guys guided evening workshop. This is very highly subscribed so do be quick, fellas, and all we ask of you is to arrive at your screen oiled and smiling. You will then be required to slowly slip down your underpants whilst gyrating to a track of our choice and then we talk you through your self-pleasuring experience, offering sexy tips and helpful remarks, sexy sounds and facial expressions – and finally marks out of ten once you (and possibly we) have climaxed. Ladies have asked if there is an equivalent for them but as neither of us are lesbians, we don't feel this is appropriate. Cardinal, however, does offer a bespoke service and can travel anywhere within the M25 and beyond. And she doesn't charge, but will pay you.

Though we are confident this book will have ensnared even the grisliest amongst you your Mr Right, we are unable to attend any resulting weddings in person, unless you are one of the many celebrities we have helped, in which case we would be delighted to join you for your big day, especially if there will be a photographer from top magazines such as *Hello!* and *Grazia*. We have been unpleasantly criticised for only attending these more upmarket weddings, but it's simply down to the fact that these people are our 'tribe', and we are more likely to have a nice time without contracting any nasty infections, and get to take away a big going-home goody bag, some unwanted wedding gifts, free food and booze and sometimes a puppy. And more often than not, furnished with the number of a reality TV star or, at the very least, the guy in charge of catering who fancies getting to know us a little bit better and comes with a phalanx of hot, firm-buttocked waiters.

Expensive gifts are, of course, always welcome, thank you, from anyone who feels they have been especially helped by us.*

* Suggested gifts include: racing driver circuit drive day out voucher with Jenson Button or similar sexy driver, with boozy sharing-picnic; Fabergé egg (at least one each please); hamper of gold or diamond jewellery (similar to Kate Middleton's or Joan Collins's); huge collection of exotic fruit in cellophane-covered basket (Fortnums only please); Ralph Lauren bedding with Ralph's signature embroidered and a shadowy smudge from his anus; sherbert lemons in expensive crystal jar; French silk underwear (size 0); Joe Wicks; long German sausage (with guy attached!); big Gucci bag of cash; two vintage cars of our choosing with champagne picnics inside; a crate of vintage champagne; expensive chocolate truffles in solid gold gift box; 68-piece monogrammed decanter and glasses set; two fur coats each; six Dyson hairdryers; an evening of kissing and cunnilingus with Leonardo DiCaprio; two weeks away at wherever George Clooney goes; a Nick Knowles makeover of two or more of our properties; a full night's massage from the young Irish chap in *Normal People*; unlimited surgery vouchers; silk, kitten-heeled Jimmy Choo day slippers (four pairs each please); a dirty weekend in a Cotswold hotel with Kevin McCloud and Alfie Boe; a plush recording studio with unlimited snacks, fizzy drinks and a flirty sound guy, to lay down some sexy close-harmonied tracks for our upcoming album *Tantalise!* with the Michaels Crawford, Bublé and Ball.

Appendix A: Ode to Mahmoud

JOAN: Frankly, we all know Mahmoud deserves a book of his own. Surgeon, musician, jockey: he has a wonderful collection of Arabian stallions that he rides at weekends and I've often joined him in my suede jodhpurs (given to me by Jane Seymour after she got too big for them) and my glitzy bolero with top hat, on a celebrity fox hunt, thundering across the hillocks on one of his studs, followed by a big spicy picnic and a big sickly pud. Being out there watching his open blouson billowing, his thigh muscles straining, his proud bottom bouncing, always brings a tear to my eye. And we generally slink off together, once the fox is down, to a secluded copse where he unpops his conkery leather satchel and releases a feast of cured meats, hot pickles and pointy baguettes for us to yum on, with a pricey wine, amidst bluebells and birdsong.

Mahmoud is one of these guys who is simply ageless. I know he gorges on avocados and creamy nuts, giving him that wonderfully soft skin that just doesn't wrinkle or jowl. When I have to go home and look at Ralph after I've been looking at Mahmoud all day, I actually feel sick. Even when he was young, Ralph had a difficult face: angular, spiky and frankly elderly looking. I've seen photos of him from his teens and at fourteen he looked like Ronnie Wood (as he is now, post-twins). I think Ralph just charmed me with his big dick energy, though as we all know, that turned out to be a terrible lie. And yes, at times I've felt very, very bitter.

Mahmoud does have a wife, but we've yet to see her, or even learn her name. God knows we've tried. I've invited them over for Christmas with their tubby triplets I don't know how many times, and he'll say 'Oh she's not well' or they're 'too busy'. You'd think she'd be some hot young supermodel or top fashion lawyer, but I worry he's actually trapped in some abusive cycle with a bedbound harridan. I do feel Mahmoud constantly battles with his spiritual desire to be good and saintly versus his profound longings of the flesh, the manly urge for complex erotic experiences and boundless romantic love he so richly deserves, which frankly he isn't going to get from his sulky, draining wife.

JERICHA: Since my cervical chapel became sadly tainted by the arrival of what Mahmoud called 'dodgy cells' in my mid-thirties – we're never sure how they got there, as they are normally associated with a high level of promiscuity – he has made it his personal crusade never to see them return, and as a result, insists on a weekly smear which he performs using his long, curly index fingernail, grown specifically for the purpose. It's a gentle but stimulating procedure, a million miles from the clattery cast-iron contraption I had to endure as a younger woman. That invasive procedure, with my legs akimbo in horse stirrups – though never 'perfectly comfortable' (in the words of Mahmoud's bumpy practice partner Sandra*) – was nevertheless endurable with a little gas and air. But this became increasingly painful as my already retrogressive womb collapsed slowly backwards, and my vaginal vestibule grew in length to a full twenty-two inches, pushing my womb higher and higher up inside my body.

Enter Mahmoud and his now renowned 'Fingering Smear'. Understandably costly, this weekly service also keeps 'the motorway ready for traffic flow' (his expression) should I feel the need for intercourse, which I do occasionally undertake with younger men, for purely medical purposes, when Phillip is stranded in Thailand sending back only wonderful photos of himself and the lads, frolicking on long sandy beaches, sadly unable to get home to penetrate his wife.

Mahmoud has, as previously mentioned, furnished me with a very useful address book of 'lengthy lads'. These chaps are all very

* See Appendix B.

polite and will pop round with a suitcase of adult toys and an eighties mix tape, throwing in a slow dance at the end if you fail to climax in the allotted time. So I certainly can't complain in that department!

A FINE-NOSED FELLOW

Such was the description afforded Mahmoud by the Duke of Cambridge when he leapt to the Duchess's aid as she fainted from a particularly heavy period, during the women's tennis final at Wimbledon one year. Mahmoud's nose is as precious and vital an organ as his heart, as it has been an indispensable medical tool for both operating and diagnosis. He didn't need to ask the reason for the Duchess's distress that day, as he picked up the tell-tale tang of a lass with the painters in, on getting within twenty feet of our swooning future Queen, thus avoiding much embarrassment for both Kath herself and her big blushing Willy. Mahmoud employs his nasal detection system to sniff out coeliacs, tumours and other nasties, and having tended to the Duchess down below, could be seen snorting about amidst the spectators, saving the lives of many of the elite enjoying their strawberries and cream, as he kindly alerted them to lurking cancers, imminent heart attacks and extramarital affairs.

By the end of the working day, Mahmoud's diagnostic nose can understandably be rather weary and start to droop, so he has designed a range of beautiful bespoke night-nose hats, to be worn in the dark, as would a kestrel at rest. As a sensual man, he loves to vary the fabrics, knowing he's going to be rubbing and fondling at his nose hat for most of the night, so boasts a stunning selection, in French silk, Austrian velvet, Yorkshire corduroy and sexy Berlin leather – swapping them around according to his nightly nose-needs.

The night-nose hat simply hooks over the end of one's hooter with a pretty ribbon secured around the back of the head like a bra. It secretes a special balm to nourish and heal the tip, promising a bright bold nose come morning.

MAN OF FASHION

There's no question Mahmoud is in a league of his own when it comes to fashion. He obviously has the height (coming in at 6ft 8in), and just the right amount of heft. And many a lady can get very damp at the sight of his broad shoulders tapering down to a slender, almost spiralling, waist, glistening into the delicately sculpted groin, ripe with frontal promise and a clearly outlined and prominent banana. Go round the back for his proud, high bottom, atop bouncy, toned thighs and calves that go on into next year. More often than not he will be wearing his freshly pressed doctor's tunic over a snug, high-end suit, his stethoscope slung casually over his shoulder like an actor's scarf.

He always wears a hat, even during surgeries and these can be anything from a velvet bowler to a hefty Stetson or a fun boater, right through to his go-to: the wee willy winky, a fun, floppy hat to cheer up angry patients coming out of anaesthesia.

Feet wise, Mahmoud never wears socks as his toes are too long (each one around nine inches) but always enjoys a bespoke backless slipper in patent party black, with just a hint of a heel. And after much pestering, he began his own footwear range for the long-toed gentleman. His sultry slipper range is popular with city gents and barrow boys alike and each pair is lovingly crafted by a team of fast-fingered women, eager simply to be near the man himself. The range includes: The Curly Slipper, Snoozy Snugglers, Scotch Parcels, Poky Pouchers and Long Leather Gentlemen, and his loafer-for-dancing collection comprises of Lattice Lover, Aubergine Orgasm, Caramel Canoe and Pushy Banana. He also has a wonderful selection of barely there underwear for big-bottomed guys in Midnight Thong, Feather Butt, Sunday Loungers, Nightwind, and Badboy Brown Breath. These are all available to order online at www.moodbymahmoud.com

His whole gorgeous persona wouldn't be complete without us referencing his extraordinarily seductive scent. Which, after huge demand from the A-listers he has treated, he has now made available to those that can afford it. We all know most male perfumes have a pungent base and ordinarily perfumiers use skunks, goat testes and so forth to achieve that 'turn-me-on' smell. But Mahmoud is never afraid to go the extra mile and for his Mr Musky range, has taken to using his own anus as the perfume starter base. Latterly, he has been experimenting as the demand for variation has increased tenfold, so he's launched a wonderfully bold collection including: Uber Driver, Fat Man with the Runs, Tubby Hubby and the slightly more sophisticated Conference Anus (available in parfum only). Chronic Conference Anus is also available as a limited edition, pure gold, purse version, and is known to be worn by guys like George Clooney and the Superman actor Henry Cavill, but it's worth knowing the guys that provided this one have all had to have anal transplants.

Appendix B: Private Lives: Our Special People

Like all leading social figures, there is always an entourage around each of us wherever we go. They are, for the most part, very nicely paid, thank you very much, and attempt to assist us in our daily lives, often shielding us from potential assassination attempts. Between us we are juggling numerous properties, ailing or distant husbands, huge-headed children and, oftentimes, wildly incompetent staff. We don't know where we'd be without them all. Thanks, guys!!!

RALPH: JOAN'S DYING HUSBAND

It goes without saying that I'm devastated to see my husband shrivelling away before my very eyes. I often weep myself to sleep as I recall our happier times as young, just-marrieds. I used to love to go shopping with Ralph in Knightsbridge; he'd slip off to buy me a surprise trouser suit or some hooker heels, and I'd grab a caramel latte to-go and hunt for jazzy silk cravats as he always hated his turkey neck (as did I). I still buy them for him now and pop them on him, but they tend to be covered in drool within half an hour.

I've no idea what the future holds as he's been in and out of that coma like a bishop in an actress. Thankfully he's over in the East Wing, and my home help Gyulchay (see below) keeps him quiet with her intimate creamings and liquidised dumplings.

Of course, I mourn things that were key to our marriage – our shared love of cattle, and some of the pricier jewellery – but given his small mouth and dry, grey tongue, his ugly face and disappointing penis, I can't say I miss our lovemaking. If anything, it's a blessed relief.

STEPHANIE: JOAN'S GHASTLY PA

Stephanie, my unwanted PA, is one of these girls with no chin to speak of and a sloppy lower lip. She lumbers about the place, her lollopy gait not helped by her unusually widthy hips. My heart sinks when I hear her hobbling along my corridor, inevitably carrying the wrong file and a tepid tea, which I'm afraid I have had to throw back in her face on more than one occasion.

I've tried time and again to give her the heave-ho, but as her mother Alison (see below) is prone to violent outbursts, I simply don't feel able to and have continued to suffer Stephanie's difficult face and oniony BO. Sometimes I put her out in the garden with Ralph, and they'll sit under a tree, the pair of them munching on mushed-up 'nanas and watching the ducks go by.

My biggest beef is that she is meant to be the face of Joan Damry, and people expect class, glamour and panache, so I'm sure I've lost huge business deals and potential modelling contracts because of her. I know there was a lot of interest in me taking over from Keira Knightley as the face of Chanel, but Stephanie forgot to get back to them. And Oprah Winfrey was going to stay one Christmas but she took one look at Stephanie, packed her Louis Vuittons and left. In honesty, I feel like I've reached a point where I may have to use my contacts in the underworld!

ALISON: STEPHANIE'S VIOLENT MOTHER

Alison and I go way back. We were friends through high school, but I was the pretty, popular one and I always got the guys. Ali could be humourous, but had no boobs to speak of and always a hint of faeces on her breath. She was known to fly into these awful rages when people said how pretty I was, and often came at me with scissors on my way home from school.

One winter I had a birthday slumber party and she spiked my hot chocolate and went at my pudenda with a blunt lady razor, leaving my vulva puffy and weeping for weeks. We all thought she'd be a spinster for life but when she finally did nab a man, it turned out they were distantly related, which I think accounts for Stephanie's appearance. I sometimes wonder if Alison's not a closet lesbian and just in love with me. It would make so much sense and she's always staring at my boobs. Seeing me having rock stars like David Coverdale on speed dial, or watching Derren Brown beg to sleep over at mine at New Year, just sent her crazy with jealousy and she got drunk and assaulted Derren on the toilet, and then said she'd kill herself if I didn't at least take on Stephanie as my PA. Awful, but I had no choice.

PIERRE: THE JACK UP JOAN'S BEANSTALK

Luckily, Pierre still lives with me and he has been an absolute blessing in my darkest hours. Having both a husband dipping in and out of a coma and a mother who refuses to go, I'm often at the end of my tether.

Pierre keeps me young and agile with our morning workouts and his bold French cuisine. Yes, we still have the beanstalk in the kitchen, growing up through the roof as I wanted that indoor-outdoor feel, and which we both climb for fitness purposes. I can't deny that as I clamber up beneath him and peek at his long heavy testes – frosted in French pubic hair and banging together like furry bells – it does give me a tremendous boost first thing.

At the end of the day, though, he is a member of staff, meaning he'll often be topless mowing the grounds on his tractor, or having his shiny brown thighs clamped around a tree, chain-sawing off some choice branches to make me a big log fire for later.

We often lounge on one of my old animal skins in front of a blazing fire come the evening, and because it's so hot I usually just wear one of my chainmail bikinis as we sup on Scotch and feed each other crackers with a big smelly cheese. Pierre has to keep really fit to maintain the castle, so I've just had a pole built in the sitting room where he likes to dance of an afternoon; it's hot work with the fire always going, so he tends to strip off as he goes. Sometimes he'll start off in a fireman's outfit or as a disgruntled *gendarme* and then boof – off comes the helmet et al and it's just him gyrating around the pole, occasionally splaying his buttocks at me to let out some heat.

GYULCHAY: JOAN'S TARTY HOME HELP

Gyulchay's origins remain shady: she could be Cuban, she could be Polish, we'll never know and she's still unable to string a sentence together despite the flash cards. I've been criticised for not paying her, but you tell me how many women from her background can say they live in a castle? She has a cosy room with the washing machines and a big old mattress beneath a wee window, and being below water level she has unlimited access to the moat, though she claims it scares her having once seen a woman's head float by.

Gyulchay's the type of lass with a very thin mouth and a somewhat haunted demeanour. But her fat boobs and toned bottom give her a confidence she doesn't really deserve, and I'm amazed at her figure considering the number of potatoes she eats, often fourteen jacket potatoes at one sitting, bursting with cottage cheese. I have to take my hat off to her with Ralph, with all the bed baths and intimate creaming, which I would find too distressing. Having not been physical with him for a long while, even before the cluster of heart attacks, I've no intention now of rubbing my palms across his crusty thighs and risking waking his angry phallus.

BRIAN: JOAN'S LOYAL DRIVER

Poor Brian's absolutely huge now, he's broken every seat in my house and always wears very tough brown trousers – he says it's because he loves autumn but I think it's more to do with his ongoing bowel issues. He knows he shouldn't continue with his big fatty breakfasts and his bumbag of pastries at 11 a.m., having lost most of his colon to giant tumours, but he loves his nosh and says when he goes, he wants a big open casket with a long Greggs sausage roll flopping out of his mouth like a greasy cigarette.

Brian still lives at home with his mother and says he's never wanted a wife because the only women he likes are Britney Spears and me. I once caught him trying to masturbate, hunched over one of my toilets, clasping a photo of me as a busty teen on a pony, but I didn't have the heart to reprimand him because he got too tired halfway through and sat down for a weep and a doughnut.

DANNY: JOAN'S SEXY SECURITY

Danny's one of these big dirty guys with twinkly blue eyes and a thick eggy voice like Frank Bruno, though his skin is white as snow. In all honesty he's really quite ginger and smells like ginger people do: that slight pepper-pong, with a hint of BO, but he masks it very nicely, thank you, with a hefty aftershave and plenty of cigarettes!

He's very bulky below and I know he sports a plump pubic bush as he says he loves to condition 'that hair', but I'll bet most of the bump is his 'man meat', as he'd call it! And I can't help but sneak a glance when it's s'clearly outlined in his clingy burgundy briefs, all huge and coiled. Danny patrols my castle in Scotland, so he's often perched atop a turret or swimming around my moat. In London he shadows me as I totter about in my stilettos to my myriad commitments, and then we'll have a big boozy lunch and a mooch in Selfridges as he loves all the chunky jewellery.

After work, we go back to my Knightsbridge pad and both love a bit of a boogie and a cheeky Prosecco before I turn in. If I'm going to bed solo, I'll slip into my silk Harrods PJs or a Lejaby thong and camisole, and Danny strips down to his satin night boxers, though he'll keep his gun on his lap and often sing me to sleep. We both love Sade, so he usually serenades me with 'Smooth Operator', which I do admit makes me tingly downstairs, especially when he dances, endlessly circling his groin with his gun tip.

JOAN SENIOR: JOAN'S DYING MOTHER

My mother, like Ralph, slips in and out of consciousness but shows no signs of departing and continues to take up most of my piano room, lazing in her glass coffin with her wee bonsai trees and microclimate, all the livelong day. She's always been a small, stout lady, but is now further shrunk in height and seemingly enwidthening day b'day, I think because Gyulchay tosses her fatty titbits whenever I'm not looking.

Like my father, she believed in firm discipline and often slapped us about with belts and slippers, so if she's getting out of line with me when she's having one of her 'sit-up' days, I've no qualms about punching her in the face.

MICK: JOAN'S HAIRDRESSER AND MAKE-UP ARTIST

Mick's stunning. Like a lot of hairdressers, he's bald, but with his big bulgy eyes you don't really notice. He's always tanned, Botoxed and beach-ready with his tight muscles and waxed chest – and yet he's not gay. He loves whizzing about my haircut on his wee stool, snipping away and poking with the tail of his comb, he's like a less fat Leonardo Da Vinci – and when he stands up to work on the top he'll always push his groin into my back to give me a taste of what he's packing.

I have Nina, Mick's sister-in-law, do my hair and make-up if I have an awards do or TV appearance because she's s'cheap and she's very good (she does everyone from Eamonn Holmes right up to the Duchess of Kent), but Nina's quite boring and very dowdy to look at, so I never let her mix with any celeb friends, although she's always loitering about with her flask and a selfie stick, so I usually give her something I don't want from my freebie goody-bag and send her on her way! Mick is my go-to when I'm down in Knightsbridge and he loves coming to my pad because I've always got a chocolate fountain on the go and he loves a dip in my infinity pool.

Not a lot of people know it, but Mick lives with AIDS although, as he says, he's not gay. Just one of those things; he thinks he got it just from shopping in Brighton, and I must say, he looks very well on it. To be honest, I'm not sure if he really has it. He's quite the drama queen and always has to have a whinge about something.

We've had the odd wee snog before, just to pass the time more than anything, but for someone so vain, I was surprised by how many teeth he had missing once I'd got my tongue inside his mouth, and I didn't much like the feel of his gummy sockets.

PHILLIP: JERICHA'S HUSBAND AND ROCK

Joan has often said Phillip and I have the perfect marriage and in many ways it's true. Phillip is a passionate charity man who spends large swathes of his time with the under-16 Boy Scout troupe he founded in Thailand. They say absence makes the heart grow fonder and, in truth, the three days a year we spend together are a kind of paradise. To have landed such a generous-hearted hunk still gives me butterflies.

During his brief sojourns home, Phillip sometimes enjoys dressing me up as a Cub – woggle, scarf and all! – and then asks me to perform rudimentary survival tasks, whilst barking instructions and taking photographs. I'll often throw together a simple supper – perhaps a fishy linguine or a mini moussaka – and we'll settle down in the sitting room, trays on laps, to re-watch *Top Gun* or *Les Mis*.

Phillip's always been quite a film buff and was very taken with the recent film version of *Cats* with Taylor Swift. And with his long list of connections to key figures in the film industry, he was able to get hold of the uncut version, where the cats still have anuses. In fact, when he's home and having one of his 'down' days, he'll shut himself in his snug and watch that on a loop.

In some ways he and my daughter Cardinal share many traits, though he is not her biological father. I, for one, have no regrets that he never sired me a child, nor paid for a single thing in our marriage. As he always says, 'You provide the funds, I do the dirty work.' As far as I'm concerned, I married a saint!

CARDINAL: JERICHA'S DRAINING DAUGHTER

It's hard to know where to start with Cardinal. Her conception was hardly the stuff of fairy tales, being the result of the over-energetic 'fumblings' of a badminton mixed-doubles partner of old. I'd had a flair for the sport at an early age and was persuaded into pairing up with my friend's partially disabled father Gerald, who plied me with G&Ts, claiming it was his birthday. I'd forgotten my track pants to slip on after the match, so was still in my flimsy white skirt when the time came for him to give me a lift home. Part-way into the journey, poor Gerald started weeping about his marriage and asked for a cuddle and then got rather carried away and asked if I'd 'suck his penis better'. I suppose nowadays it might be called an assault, but we knew back then it was just a bit of horseplay and the result of me carelessly cavorting about in rather too short a skirt!

A competent badminton player despite having one leg much shorter than the other, Gerald was a wide, simple-looking man with afro-type hair, though he was white (looking back it was probably a tight perm), and a no-nonsense attitude, particularly when shouting 'MINE' on court and off. Joan always says he looked like Fred West who, all things considered, was not a bad-looking guy.

The resulting pregnancy was almost intolerable due to the size of Cardinal's head permanently putting a kink in my spine as it grew out in every direction. And the birth itself was so traumatic I vowed never to have another child, which was fine by Phillip whom I met shortly after. It's curious, really, when he has such affinity with the young, and when he shows me videos of himself with the young Thai boys clambering all over him, it sometimes brings a tear to my eye.

Cardinal has been the bane of my life for thirty-four years. She's caused me countless embarrassments, huge financial losses through endless fines and bail costs, not to mention all the camera equipment she's demanded I buy for an art project which turned out to be her up-skirting spree, lasting nine months until the police finally caught up with her on a remote Scottish island. They know her very well at our local police station and the female bobbies have been so patient – they often allow her to pop in for a hot shower before going bowling with them or for a bite.

Mahmoud has submitted Cardinal to endless testing (some voluntary, some under enforced anaesthesia), but in the end the best diagnosis he has been able to reach is to describe her as 'A Walking Syndrome'.

FANNY DOMAIN: JERICHA'S BOXER MOTHER

I was born in Tunbridge Wells to Fanny Domain, a fiery redhead who pulled me out two months early, using her own bare hands. She had moved from Ilkley to Tunbridge shortly before I was born, having bitten a man's nose off in a pub brawl over some cheese and onion crisps. As a much-feared boxer, she was always quick to anger, but sought to channel that aggression into local county fights, competing at the National Women's Boxing Championship when she was five months pregnant with me.

When my parents were first together, she was in awe of my father

Donald's height and enjoyed the way he would toss her around the room during lovemaking. But as her boxing prowess grew, the tables turned, and though she was only 4ft 5in she would be the one spinning the 6ft 6in Donald around, which began to take its toll on his self-esteem.

I became her key focus, as she hoped I might follow in her boxing footsteps, attempting to train me by often punching me in the face in the middle of the night. Unfortunately, due to my very long feet and rather gentle nature, I simply wasn't cut out for the pugilist lifestyle and this sent Mother into a terrible fury. She visited the local pub and, after a game of darts and fifteen pints, got into an altercation with a local farmer, who bet his farm against our squalid two-up two-down if she fought his prime bullock. Fanny, of course, rose to the challenge but was sadly mauled, her body parts strewn across several fields. Thus, when she departed this world, we were homeless and my father was deemed unfit to look after me. But I was fortunate enough to land on my feet, having already been betrothed by Mother to my first (and much older) husband, Randy Cork. Randy was already a grandfather when we met and sadly died very suddenly soon after we were married, found with a pillow inexplicably taped to his face and poison in his veins, leaving me his not inconsiderable fortune. I reverted to my mother's maiden name Domain at that point, in fond memory of tough old Fanny – and have hung on to it ever since.

DR GRAHAM NUPP: JERICHA'S CLOSE FRIEND

Graham and I first met when I was doing a post-grad gynae-psyche course at Cambridge and he had just become a consultant at a wonderful private hospital nearby. I initially met him at the medical choir we'd both joined; I was an unexpected baritone, he a borderline soprano, but we'd only exchanged smiles during our intimate vocal warm-ups where we had to grab our groins and grunt, which made us both blush!

I met him again a few weeks later, as a patient. And I can't deny, during our consultation about some of my own gynae issues (indeed he was the person responsible for first discovering my 22-inch-long vaginal canal, because on attempting a smear he lost three speculums up there), I was very taken by his wiry physique, quick wit and freckly Celtic skin. After the examination he found an excuse to follow me to the hospital canteen where he bought me a coffee and a bun (also being quick to diagnose early coeliac disease due to the chronic wind I suffered post-bun).

We soon began dating, enjoying lots of hearty rambles with veggie picnics, heady nights at the theatre (alight with intellectual discussions about Shakespeare and Pinter), and frenzied tap dancing on his rooftop patio after too much champagne! Graham was also rather perfect physically, light framed, with a very slender but long penis (17 inches) which I found perfectly sufficient for my requirements, but since he couldn't fill my entire 22-inch vestibule, he began to feel inadequate, often slipping it up my back passage instead, which he seemed to enjoy much more, and gradually our courting fizzled out. He went on to marry and quickly divorce a rather brutish German woman and has remained single ever since.

We regularly meet at his book group, where he always finds a reason to make me stay behind – and after a spillage on his cords at the last one, he had to take them off, so once again I was able to witness his still-handsome trouser worm as it slipped out of his boxers and down his thigh and onto his ankle. Being so long, when it does become engorged it rises in a manner more akin to a snake being charmed from its basket, curling up, up and away! Joan has often encouraged me to rekindle my and Graham's connection, but he's pretty busy with all his clinics and a rather giggly new Dutch flatmate called Jacco – and in any case I don't feel I should, given the kind of fairytale marriage Phillip and I share.

MARK: JERICHA'S HAIRDRESSER AT NICKY CLARKE

Mark knows my hair so well. I've been going to him for twenty-five years now and I don't even have to tell him what I want any more. Each new haircut is just a wonderful surprise, but always based around the same haircut: the Judi Dench feathered-cap cut, which he does on all his clients and himself. Whilst working away on my head, Mark always turns the chair round so I can't cheat and peep in the mirror as he's slash-cutting and chipping into whatever he's inspired to do that day.

He wears a pretty heavy, perfumed crotch scent that they sell over the counter at Nicky's (I always get a bottle to take home for Phillip who thoughtfully saves it for 'when I'm with my Thai boys'), so I get a good nose slug of that when Mark's clambering onto the arms of the hairdresser's chair to get a good view of my barnet, as he likes to call it (originating as he does from Epping). It's pretty active, hot and sweaty work for him, though, so by the time he leans in for his final 'high blow blast' finish, I get quite a heady burst of fresh 'n' funky groin waft, which I can't deny is wonderfully intoxicating. Then he leaps down, tears off his shirt and spins me round to see the finished cut. And I always love it!

MARIO: JERICHA'S TAILOR

I was first introduced to Mario by Joan. Now in his eighties, he still works tirelessly from his little offices in Soho and I'll often phone him on a Sunday night to say I need a fancy trouser suit by Monday morning for a telly appearance – and I know he'll be up all night, his chubby old fingers whizzing up and down seams with just the flash of the needle and a wisp of cigar ash as he pants away to bring the item to fruition.

His son Alonzo makes me a herbal tea for my arrival, and always manages a quick grope of my boobs when he's doing my fitting! I don't mind at all, it's nice to know there are still some men with blood in their veins.

Like Joan, I love to have all my clothing made bespoke and more recently have been looking to Mario for my tankinis. For many years I wore the same one, often patching over the torn gusset with old bits of plimsoll, or the fingers of my rubber gloves. But Mario says he wants me to feel beautiful when I plough up and down my dirty waterways, and when himself and Alonzo are all over me with their tape measures and hot Italian fingers, it transports me to a bygone era when women were women and men were men.

Mario was also responsible for fashioning my nipple inserts due to my heavily inverted teats, and if he sends a parcel (or often Alonzo delivers it on his motorbike) there's always a handwritten note and some salami in clingfilm, that just says, 'I care.'

SANDRA: MAHMOUD'S 'PARTNER' IN HIS PRACTICE

Sandra doesn't really deserve a mention, except to say what a nasty piece of work she is. She often tries to book me in with her for my weekly smear and then batters me about, clanking and bashing me with the speculum, rather than allowing Mahmoud to insert a willowy finger up my elongated front passage.

She's wheedled her way into Mahmoud's life and practice, and both Joan and I feel sure she forged her certificates to get there. She's a stout, bullish woman with peppery breath and angry nipples that positively buck out of her starched white coat at one when entering her 'office'. She knows Mahmoud is married but follows him round like a bad fart and insists on being present at all his consultations.

She's also the type of woman who thinks it's OK to have a short manly haircut and wear next to no make-up. Neither of us feel she represents Mahmoud's practice properly; he needs someone glossy and glamorous drifting around in heavy perfume, who will seduce people with her lilting voice and sassy hip-sway. Sandra thumps about on her low heels with a smug smile and a face like a bulldog chewing a wasp.

Acknowledgements

Obviously when it comes to gratitude and thanking the right people, it's nice to have someone else blow one's trumpet, but there are occasions where one must blow oneself! So blow we shall, and give ourselves two very hearty pats on our slender backs, for writing what's likely to become as much a part of literary history and top Russell Group university education as any Brönte or Austen novel. Indeed, the Bible itself may well find it has a run for its money in terms of the sheer heft of worldwide impact this text will inevitably have upon the needy and the broken.

Thank you, Joan. Thank you, Jericha. You're welcome.

That said, we wouldn't have been able to craft such a tome without our 'writers all nighters' alongside our spiritual 'husband', Mahmoud and his esteemed ginger-lidded colleague, Dr Graham Nupp, sharing roast pigs on spits, pricey Ottolenghi salads and heavenly vintage wines from Graham's seemingly endless cellar! A shout-out must also go out too to the furious broadcaster Jeremy Paxman for all the jacket potatoes! Watching his deft tongue ploughing into a prawn-packed potty always moistened our lady caverns); thanks also to Wendy Craig for her bottomless basket of gorgeous homemade eggy hair conditioner; Princess Anne for the pretty hair clips and a pair of very soiled jodhpurs; Robert Kilroy Silk for the boozy weekends away at his Cotswold bolthole (don't ask!);

Oprah Winfrey for her precise script editing and gentle reprimands; Michelle Obama for the huge box of luminous nail varnishes; Sir David Attenborough for all the naughty knickers; Melvyn Bragg for the curling tongs and home-churned butter; 'Ye West for his wise words and weekend trouser range; Stormzy for inspiring our moist shortbread collection and, of course, the shy Dragon Peter Jones for the whispery phone lullabies and misty blue-eyed looks across the corner cafe table at John Lewis ... Thank you!

Might we also take this opportunity to praise simply ALL the wonderful men who've crossed our paths, both literally and sexually. Without you guys we would have stumbled and fallen at the very first hurdle! So what if you slipped a finger in an unsuspecting gusset as you helped us to our feet, or brushed a bumpy groin across a girlish face as you raced to help yet another ditsy maiden on her knees! We're grateful for all those doors you held open and the botty pats you dished out, as we passed through them in our kitten heels.

We are, forever and always, your humble servants.

Joan Damry and Jericha Domain